Parenting With the Beatitudes

PARENTING WITH THE BEATITUDES

Eight Holy Habits for Daily Living

Jeannie and Ben Ewing

TAN Books
Charlotte, North Carolina

Cover design by Caroline K. Green

Cover image: Multicolored toy building blocks, by Bangkok Click Studio / Shutterstock

Library of Congress Control Number: 2018967330

ISBN: 978-1-5051-1304-4

Published in the United States by
TAN Books
PO Box 410487
Charlotte, NC 28241
www.TANBooks.com

Printed in the United States of America

To our three beautiful girls who teach us so much about life and love, and to our baby boy who is a blessing and gift to us all

CONTENTS

Introduction

The Beatitudes

Blessed are the poor in spirit,
for theirs is the kingdom of heaven.
Blessed are they who mourn,
for they will be comforted.
Blessed are the meek,
for they will inherit the land.
Blessed are they who hunger and thirst for righteousness,
for they will be satisfied.
Blessed are the merciful,
for they will be shown mercy.
Blessed are the clean of heart,
for they will see God.
Blessed are the peacemakers,
for they will be called children of God.
Blessed are they who are persecuted for the sake of righteousness,
for theirs is the kingdom of heaven.
Blessed are you when they insult you and persecute you
and utter every kind of evil against you [falsely] because
of me. Rejoice and be glad, for your reward will be great
in heaven.

—Matthew 5:3–12

Beloved, timeless, and poignant for all people in every circumstance of life, the Beatitudes have become the basis for countless homilies, books, and spiritual enrichment workshops. As children, most of us had to memorize and recite them in religion class, and as adults, they are written on our hearts. What else grants such encouragement like the Beatitudes? When we are hopeless, the Beatitudes remind us of the gift of suffering. When we are discouraged, they encourage us to persevere in the face of trials.

There's no one-size-fits-all for parenting. Despite the plethora of parenting books on the market today, none can be universally applied to every parent and every child. Most of them are "how-to" books that describe techniques for improving behavior. But the one common downfall of many books on the secular market today is this: they don't address rooting out vice and fostering virtue.

We feel that the Beatitudes are a perfect framework for doing just that. They are clear and distinct from one another, yet they are also cohesive and one concept overlaps another beautifully. The Beatitudes guide both parents and children on a path to holiness, a path we believe families can—and should—take together. They show us a way of life, not just a specific strategy. And they address the underlying cause of common frustrations in the home: fighting, selfishness, jealousy, loneliness, anger, and such.

Different Bible translations offer alternative synonyms to the word "blessed" in each beatitude. Some say "happy" are they who mourn. Others say "beloved." It's likely that most of us, when we are struggling as parents, don't want to hear that we are happy when we suffer and mourn or are blessed in some way (though it is true). But to hear that we are beloved, that we are eternally loved by God? That's something altogether consoling, isn't it?

As parents, we often face times of discouragement, trials, and suffering. When we cradle our newborns, we can't foresee the crosses of parenthood. Instead, we bask in the soothing coos, smiles, and precious tiny little feet and hands. Yet, as any parent knows, the challenges do arrive in some form or another. We encounter tantrums when our children enter the "terrible twos" (or "threes" in our case). During the school years, we deal with flippant attitudes, back-talking, and disrespect. Adolescence tries our patience and willpower in ways only parents of teens can really understand.

The drama, the crises, and the selfishness—every parent faces these, and many more, impediments to rearing children. Nothing makes us more keenly aware of the effects of original sin than watching children grow. Our children often resist obedience or refuse to choose what's right, good, and true. We've come to realize, especially as parents of two girls with very different special needs, that no handbook will adequately prepare any parent to raise a child perfectly.

But we can learn to change *ourselves* as parents. We can discern, by growing in virtue ourselves, how to train our children similarly. If there's any truth in the age-old clichés, this one rings truest of all: Our children model their behavior after our own when we demonstrate and actively teach them each virtue. And each of the Beatitudes contains within it several virtues that both we, as parents, and our children can learn to grow and live more fully every day.

As we have found in our family, the Beatitudes are the ideal place to begin if we truly wish to carry the crosses of parenthood with grace. Because men and women view the world through different lenses and tend to parent according to that worldview, we decided to co-author this book so that both moms and dads could glean some wisdom on their journey of parenthood.

Parenthood is no easy task, especially in our modern era. We battle so many of the world's enticements: the glitz and glamor of having more stuff; the thrill of instant gratification by way of our technological devices (which also provide distractions); the interminable message from society through mass media about finding happiness by pursuing what we want and what makes us feel good; pervasive spiritual apathy, etc. There are endless examples, but the point is that, as Christians, we are called to be countercultural.

How do we do this? The Beatitudes provide very specific clues. We learn that, in our difficulties of dealing with fighting kids, outbursts of anger and jealousy, gnawing impatience, and the complexities of living in a world that promotes tolerance as its highest good, we can turn to the consolation provided in the Beatitudes. Again and again, their enduring message turns our focus to the scope of helping our spouse and children attain heaven rather than pleasing the world in which we live by trying to fit in.

Each chapter dives deeply into one of the eight Beatitudes, looking at them both in light of our growth as parents and as they relate to our children's growth. We investigate the virtues that relate to each beatitude and suggest ways we can foster those in our daily lives. Each of these sections is followed by reflections from us, Jeannie and Ben. We then offer a simple action plan for your family, and we conclude with a short prayer.

In his welcoming address at World Youth Day in 2002, St. John Paul II offered these promising words for those of us who are truly striving to live out our call to holiness as spouses and parents: "The joy promised by the Beatitudes is the very joy of Jesus himself: a joy sought and found in obedience to the Father and in the gift of self to others." We've learned that suffering, when offered in the true spirit of love, does beget joy. And this is the joy we hope to share with you through the ups and downs, questions and confusion, and celebrations and triumphs of the journey of parenthood.

We can't promise you the golden book on parenting tips, but we can promise that you can change your family dynamic when you first change *yourself*. We've found this to be true firsthand, and we're not saints (yet)! Parenting doesn't necessarily get easier as time progresses, but it does get better. This book can be a companion to you as you navigate the messes and fights, silent treatments and heartbreaks, and distractions and setbacks of parenting your children. Let's face this beautiful cross and discover how challenges can change us for the better.

CHAPTER 1

Blessed Are the Poor in Spirit, for Theirs Is the Kingdom of Heaven

The family is the first and most essential of all Christian communities. Where can we better experience our own poverty and that of others than in the closely shared life of a couple and family members?

—Father Jacques Philippe[1]

Jeannie

My understanding of poverty has evolved over the past year or so. Like most people, when I heard the word "poor," my mind conjured up images of the homeless and people in shelters or soup kitchens. Sadly, my concept of poverty was limited to socioeconomic status. Yet I have since learned that poverty can take many forms—spiritual, emotional, material, etc. True *Gospel* poverty, however, is

---

[1] Jacques Philippe, *The Eight Doors to the Kingdom: Meditations on the Beatitudes* (Scepter, 2018), 18.

a lifestyle choice and has nothing to do with the socioeconomic status one is born into. To be "poor in spirit" is a gift, a virtue, a grace essentially. God calls certain people to a particular level of simplicity that extends beyond that which most of us understand or desire.

Here is a reflection by Jean Vanier found in the September 27, 2013 issue of the *Magnificat* periodical, which is another piece of wisdom that can expand our view of what poverty is and who are the poor among us.

> Through baptism, each person's heart belongs to God. Some people, however, are called to manifest this gift of their belonging in a special way and through a particular way of life. The Gospels seem to reveal to us another aspect of consecration: the mystery of the poor consecrated to God through the sacred "oils" of pain, rejection, and weakness. When Paul says that God has chosen the weak, the foolish, and the rejected, or when Jesus, in Matthew's Gospel, describes the Kingdom of God as a wedding feast to which all the poor, the lame, the sick, and the blind are invited, they confirm that the weak have a preferential place in the heart of God. Jesus himself was rejected and outcast; he identifies with the rejected, the outcasts. Is that not the Gospel's new order that replaces the old? We in L'Arche are beginning to touch something of the mystery that people like St. Vincent de Paul grasped when he said: "The poor are our teachers."

Vanier does not mean to say that exclusion or rejection are in accordance with God's will. On the contrary! They are the fruits of sin and hardness of heart. The Gospel shows, however, that God welcomes in a special way those whom society rejects.

My daughter Sarah is an example of one who is poor. She was born with a craniofacial anomaly and other physical differences. She has undergone a major surgery to modify her skull so that her brain has room to grow. She is in pain at times, a pain some of us who are well into adulthood may never experience ourselves. She is poor.

Being poor should not lend a negative connotation. We should not view the poor shamefully. In fact, we should *seek to be poor ourselves.* Being poor in spirit means that we are empty; we acknowledge our nothingness, sinfulness, and weakness. And in so doing, we hand over our pride, hardened hearts, fears, and facades to God. It is only when we become empty of *ourselves* that God can fill us with his love and thus fulfill his beautiful purpose in our lives.

People like Sarah, those with physical or psychological disabilities, are born poor in spirit. There is an honesty and authenticity about them so rare that it has become a treasure to many. The poor teach the rest of us, because they have nothing to hide from the world. They possess nothing, and they know that. Their poverty is evident and visible; it is impossible to hide from the world.

While most of us live in comfort and seek wealth and status, the poor have become accustomed to discomfort, pain, and suffering. That is their way of life, and yet many of them—in their vulnerability—make us uncomfortable. We're uncomfortable because we do not want to face the poverty in ourselves; we cover up our struggles and sins and instead show the world our "happy face." We allow the world to believe in a lie about ourselves, which sometimes we come to believe as well. This delusion is not uncommon. But the poor remind us that we are like them. We, too, are lacking in something. Perhaps it is not in money or socioeconomic status or education. Perhaps our poverty is in the secrets and darkness we are tempted to hide. Perhaps we are poor because we do not have God. We do not have faith. So our poverty is due to the void we feel each day, because we do not experience God's goodness and grace.

We can be humbled in the sight of the poor and suffering, the babies and the elderly, and those with physical and cognitive differences. When I look into Sarah's eyes and see such great love, my heart is pierced with the understanding that I lack love and am quite selfish. When I see a homeless man hanging his head in shame, I'm reminded that I am like that man on the inside, ashamed of my own poverty that I'm able to hide, but which he cannot.

God often humbles us and allows us to be humiliated, and we should be grateful for these humiliations, because they are opportunities for us to grow in grace and sanctification. Humiliations, such as those incidents in which we are ignored, overlooked, or criticized, may feel shameful but, in fact, are disguised gifts from God. If we accept them graciously, we will grow in poverty of spirit.

May the poor be always beautiful to us. May we strive to be like them. May we desire to share in their suffering, because suffering is a common thread in humanity. They are representatives of God, because they are not afraid to be real, to allow their misery and strife to be visible. Sarah was born that way, unashamed of who she is and how she was created to look differently than most of us. In turn, I am the one who has learned from her and continue to be amazed when I see highly educated professionals tell me how much she has touched their hearts.

That is the gift of grace that is evident in the poor. Even if we are not materially or intellectually poor, we can be spiritually poor. This poverty is not contingent upon socioeconomic status or cognitive aptitude; rather, it's based upon an intense desire to become empty of every distraction and excess that gets in the way of allowing God to be all that we need.

When we reach a point in which our awareness of personal weaknesses creates an immediate longing and dependency on God, then we are on the way to becoming poor in spirit. The key here is not to allow our failures and frailties to cause despondency in us; on the contrary, we look upward in our humiliated condition, and we allow God to do with us as he wishes.

Children are naturally poor in spirit. As they grow older and become more cynical because of life experiences, betrayals, or various other disappointments, the evidence of this heart-gift fades over time. As parents, we have to grasp that short window of opportunity when they are still in their formative years to point out and encourage the moments we notice their simple wisdom, untainted by the world's stain and the complexity of difficult emotions.

Simplicity

What does it mean to be poor in spirit specifically as a *parent?* In part, it means that we learn from our children, that we are open to the wisdom that can be discovered in their purity and innocence. As adults, we complicate things and overanalyze. Because of this, we often miss the simple ways God speaks to us, often through our own children. They are not jaded by sin as small youngsters, so they recognize God in his splendor—through the flowers, in the bird's evensong, from a stranger's smile.

Being poor in spirit involves an emptying of our adult complexities, as mentioned earlier. When we hand God our distractions, schedules, finances, worries, and multifaceted lives, we are allowing him to empty us so that we can see his glory more clearly and honestly. This type of spiritual poverty results in our ability to rediscover beauty in the small and simple joys that each day offers us, and we can share these moments with our sons and daughters.

I recall one lazy summer afternoon with my oldest daughter, Felicity. We were sauntering down the neighborhood sidewalk on our way to the post office in our sleepy rural town. As usual, I had a million things weighing on my mind: *What medical bills await us today? Am I getting my paycheck in the mail? I wonder how much we owe on my student loans? Will there be enough money left over for groceries?*

At the time, we were struggling from the financial strain of caring for a medically fragile child, our middle daughter, Sarah. Medical bills were pouring in each day, some for smaller amounts, but many for hundreds, even thousands, of dollars. That's where my mind was as I walked hand in hand with Felicity, but she taught me a profound lesson in spiritual poverty that day.

"Mama," she began with a peaceful smile, "do you see those flowers? Look at all the colors, Mama!" I stopped with her and nodded in agreement. "Did you know that God made all the flowers, because he loves us so much?" she added. That question stunned and humbled me. Her acknowledgment of God's gift to us in something so simple was a stark reminder that I was worrying about transitory things rather than finding God's touch of love in the flowers.

All of my worries melted away in that moment, and in that emptying, I was filled with the fruits of peace and joy. My little four-year-old daughter brought me back to the source—God—so that I would be centered and immersed in him rather than in my own daily struggles.

That's the beauty of this beatitude. We don't have to maintain any sort of pretenses in order to live fruitfully. In fact, God asks the opposite of us. He wants us to shed our facades and become like children again. As our hearts are fashioned into childlike love, we connect with our children in a powerful way. Because they see the world through poverty of spirit, we begin to speak their language when we become empty ourselves.

That heart language is what children remember most. In the daily connections we make with our kids, usually over something simple and perhaps even mundane, they learn from us as they do from God. Their openness to God's whispers and hidden gifts brings us to a place in our own lives where we reconnect with our own childhood innocence.

Poverty of spirit and simplicity share a particular kinship, because one necessarily leads to the other. For example, we have learned a few key points about spiritual poverty: it is not contingent upon one's social status, wealth, or intellect; it requires an outpouring of all extraneous diversions that keep us separated from God; and it involves an emptying of self in order that God might fill us with himself.

Simplicity needs this emptying in order to thrive. When we become less complicated and perhaps require less in terms of daily comforts, food preferences, and all the particulars that comprise our persnickety way of living, then our hearts become more satisfied with fewer material things.

When this happens, the pull toward simplicity becomes much more prominent. We find ourselves wanting fewer material possessions, purchasing less at the stores, maybe even eating simpler, more wholesome foods. We aren't picky about clothing or hairstyles or digital devices. Instead, these things begin to fall by the wayside. It is a chiseling of the heart in which God assists us in shedding the desire for achieving the ever-elusive and nonexistent American Dream.

As our hearts are molded and shaped, we see with fresh eyes. Our worldview becomes more aligned with God's. We see our mission and purpose as parents and as a family in a much clearer, succinct light. Secular pursuits have lost their luster, and we, in turn, find ourselves lured more and more by a thirst for seeking the kingdom of God *first* in our lives.

Simplicity replaces all our mental, emotional, material, and even digital clutter when we take steps toward making God the king of our home and family. Self-mortification is a perfect place to begin because when we deny ourselves the typical comforts to which we are accustomed, the soul becomes stronger. We are content with less. Rich and poor no longer describe how well dressed or financially successful we are. They become descriptors of our interior condition. We understand, through becoming poor in spirit, that we can be rich in what matters to God and yet poor by societal standards.

Growing in Holiness as a Family

What can we do as families to live out the beatitude of growing in spiritual poverty and simplicity? Most likely spiritual poverty doesn't mean we will be joining the monastic life, but we can still live in the world and yet be set apart in some way, by the way we live.

As parents, we need to be heavily cognizant of our lifestyle. Are we encouraging our children to live with fewer toys, books, and things in general? Do we frequently discuss what we wish we possessed, yet do not? Are we jealous of those who have more material goods than we do? (Here we can see how an examination of conscience regarding the Ten Commandments is helpful.)

It's difficult, but critical, that we keep our eyes, hearts, and hands heavenward. We are competing against the world, yes, and against our children's peers who may have "more" than they do. But we have to keep pointing out the beauty of living with less, because it leaves so much more room to ponder and pray about the sublimity of heaven. That's not to say we all sit and gaze at a crucifix all day. Rather, it means that our hearts are like compasses pointed north. Regardless of life's twists and turns, we are guided by our consciences that lead us toward heaven.

In many homes, growing in this beatitude may include regular visits to the homeless shelter, volunteering once a month at a local soup kitchen, or helping out with your parish's St. Vincent de Paul food pantry. Maybe you'll decide to hold a monthly clean-up day, in which everyone pitches in to clean the house and donate toys, books, and clothing in good condition.

Birthdays and other holidays, such as Christmas, can also be a glut for our kids. Foster gratitude in them by restricting gifts to three, maximum. We call this the "three gifts of the wise men" in our home. Children select one item they need (e.g., new socks, shoes, a coat), one they want (a new toy, movie, or book), and something they can do as a family (movie tickets, a zoo pass, or board game).

Another way to cultivate a spirit of poverty is to discuss how your children can be an example of generosity toward the poor on special feast days or holidays. Consider suggesting to your children that, instead of birthday presents, they request family and friends bring donations for your church's food pantry or a monetary donation to the charity of their choice. Such a request allows a different lifestyle practice than what the world suggests, because your children will see the indelible value of giving more and living with less.

The gift of this beatitude is twofold. One, we become less and less filled with frivolities and extraneous complexities that distract us from authentic living. That emptying-of-self results in a spiritual depth that changes who we are and how we approach each day. Instead of hurrying through life, instead of chasing the American Dream, instead of becoming impatient with our children, we pause just long enough to see the world as they do.

The second gift is that our children notice a change of heart in us. They see our willingness to speak at their level and, more importantly, to listen. They recognize our intentional choices to do without, sacrifice, and be generous to others in most need.

Spiritual Poverty of the Blessed Mother

The Blessed Mother lived each of the Beatitudes perfectly, of course, but poverty of spirit proved to be the primary blessing of her life. Born to both socioeconomic poverty and gifted with the virtue of simplicity, Our Lady's unstained soul made room for the perfection of this beatitude. We read about the wisdom of being poor in spirit in the Canticle of Mary, otherwise known as the Magnificat prayer, in Luke 1:46–55:

> And Mary said:
>   "My soul proclaims the greatness of the Lord;
>   my spirit rejoices in God my savior.
>   For he has looked upon his handmaid's lowliness;
>   behold, from now on will all ages call me
>   blessed.
>   The Mighty One has done great things for me,
>   and holy is his name.
>   His mercy is from age to age
>   to those who fear him.

He has shown might with his arm,
dispersed the arrogant of mind and heart.
He has thrown down the rulers from their
thrones
but lifted up the lowly.
The hungry he has filled with good things;
the rich he has sent away empty.
He has helped Israel his servant,
remembering his mercy,
according to his promise to our fathers,
to Abraham and to his descendants forever."

Here, she calls herself lowly, or poor. She describes the greatness of God by proclaiming that he scatters those who are proud and allows the rich to experience some sort of emptiness, presumably material. This canticle fulfills the words of her Son, who said, "The last will be first, and the first will be last" (Mt 20:16).

Lowliness, in God's eyes, is considered the perfection of the soul. Littleness, a simple wisdom of childlike faith, and a heart that is receptive to God's good gifts are all effects of this beatitude—effects the Blessed Mother used to raise her Son.

Mothers are born with receptive hearts. We open ourselves to the vulnerability of love when we receive our husbands in marriage and then again when we receive the seed of new life in our wombs. Our bodies expand to allow another little human to grow, and so must our hearts. If pregnancy means that we allow the space in our wombs to be filled, then this is the ultimate form of spiritual receptivity. Along with it, our hearts become open to the gift discovered in a life of sacrifice.

Being poor in spirit as a mother, if we are to model it after Our Lady, means that we are willing to enter into the cross of motherhood and all it may entail: losing a child to death prematurely; allowing a son or daughter to experience skinned knees, a broken heart, necessary surgery, ostracism from peers; or the grown-up problems of divorce, bankruptcy, and addiction.

Like the Blessed Mother, we will watch our children suffer as they grow up, and we suffer alongside them. But we remain open, receptive, and willing to undergo the pain of loss and change, because it paves the path for our—and their—sanctification.

Ben

Let's face some facts. As men, we don't want to be poor in *anything*. That may be why our pride can blind us to even *contemplating* this beatitude. We certainly don't want to admit that we need any help, especially when it comes to directions. (How could we possibly lose our way? We're guys, and we know exactly where we're going!) The truth is we *don't* always know where we're going, and this lack of direction most certainly translates into our spiritual lives.

As fathers, we can quickly distract ourselves with work, chores around the house, kids getting into trouble, and a countless array of other needs that vie for our attention. The peeling paint, small stains on the carpet, or the light fixture that needs to be replaced (among other things around the home) begin to chip away at the time we use for prayer.

By doing all of these ordinary daily activities, we can begin to lose sight of our need for God in all areas of our lives. We want to take care of our families and homes as husbands and fathers, and God wants to take care of us in the same way. It's in the act of recognizing how poor we are *without* God, in humility, that we realize our desperate situation.

Christ asks us to become like children, not childish as our inclination may be, and we begin to link being poor in spirit with this command from Jesus. Just as our children trust us to protect and provide, so also should we lean on God to protect and provide for *us*. We certainly need to realize that we should still be the hands and feet of Jesus, but we are only able to act *because of* the life he has given us.

Think about that: God has breathed life into us, and without his action, we would not exist. After pondering this, we can begin to grasp the enormity of God's essence, and this overshadowing turns into awe—like how our small children are in awe of how tall or strong we are.

The awe of God (e.g., fear of the Lord) and his infinite character place us in a quiet frame of mind, which is certainly something to contemplate. In order to be better parents, we should know our place in the pecking order of life, which can become difficult. When curious children ask simple questions with complex answers, we begin to ad-lib answers as best as we can. If we are not careful, we can become "experts" in everything, and soon pride creeps in like an invisible barrier between us and God. It's okay not to know every answer to every question our kids ask, and the honesty we show our children will shine through in our marriages and, ultimately, with God in the confessional. To be poor in answers points the direction to our inmost spiritual poverty by helping us to realize our dependence on God and the two thousand years of wisdom the Catholic Church has stored up for us to tap into.

By showing our children that we do not have all the answers to life's questions, we can begin to understand how crucial it is to show them how to find answers through prayer and studying our Catholic faith. Our poverty of spirit then shines through our guidance in such a way that we can be honest enough with our children to say, "I don't have an answer for you, but let's look it up together." Admitting our ignorance allows spiritual poverty to become the guiding step on a journey through learning the faith with your children together. Sometimes our children ask deeply profound questions, and it's up to us to show how truly poor in spirit we are by admitting, "I don't know," and following it up with, "but let's find out together."

To be poor in answers is to be rich in humility.

Reflecting back on a point where humility is a sharp and stark reality for me, I immediately think of my middle daughter, Sarah, who was born with a rare genetic disorder. On the day of her birth, I was fairly carefree. We had gone through one birth before, so the whole process seemed familiar, and there was very little anxiety on my part. (Of course, I had no idea what was waiting for me at the end of a very long day.)

The birth started out as normal with Jeannie's contractions, breathing steadily, and waiting for the right time to begin the birthing process. I thought that it would be over quickly, but then everything changed. No matter how hard my wife tried to push, our stubborn kid would not come out. After twenty-six hours of waiting, my wife was pushing to the point of exhaustion (and some tears and frustration), and our doctor said it was time for a C-section.

This was not what either of us had envisioned for that day, and a large part of my fear was certainly wondering what Jeannie would have to go through. Still, we had no idea the day could offer any more surprises at that point, and everyone thought the end was in sight. Once Jeannie had been prepped for surgery and was ready for the C-section, I sat near her head with a curtain up. I tried my best to keep her calm, but for the life of me, I can't recall what I said.

Once I heard the screams of our daughter, I knew that both Jeannie and Sarah would be fine. As the doctors cleaned up Sarah and brought her around the side of the curtain, I saw her hands for the first time and was aghast. She had no individual fingers, so—stupefied—I averted my gaze to her face. It appeared to be different than a typical newborn's face, and her forehead was bruised from being lodged in the birth canal. At that point, my world fell apart, and the exhaustion of the day overwhelmed me.

The doctor came over to me and asked, "Does your family have any history of genetic disorders?" I quickly said, "No," but then my thoughts began to race through my head: *Will she survive? What's wrong with her? Will she be intelligent? Will she struggle her whole life? Can her hands and feet be fixed with surgery?*

With so many questions, I felt as though the excitement of being a new father was felled with the reality of a child who would always be *different*. I was faced with a stark choice:

unconditionally love Sarah for who she is, or be resentful towards God for not sending me a "normal" child. Removing all my preconceived notions of who this child would grow up to be, and knowing that God had intended more for her and our family than I thought possible, I had to place myself in the mind of Jesus and love her for who she is, not for who I expected her to be.

Just as Jesus spent time with the lowliest outcasts of society, I was given the chance to humble myself and accept and love this child, a child who society might consider to be abnormal and disfigured. It was a day that forever changed me, and I thank God that I had the grace to love Sarah with an open heart. If the Lord had not ground down my will over the course of twenty-six hours the day Sarah was born, I would not have been open to his will.

God loves us despite our shortcomings, and this constant love should be a great relief to us as fathers. We try to love unconditionally, but it is a very real challenge. On some days, one child may be better behaved than another, which may factor into unintentionally playing favorites. And, if we're honest with ourselves, we do this constantly. God plays favorites too; we're *each* his favorite child!

The more active our prayer life, the more we begin to realize how much spiritual progress we lack. Once again, it's okay to say that our prayer life is lacking. It's a step forward in spiritual poverty and recognition of that fact. Just as your children ask for mercy when they are disciplined, so, too, should we be asking for mercy and an outpouring of God's grace into our lives. Asking for mercy is never easy, and no one should tell you that it is. Just be open to the stripping of pride in your life, recognize the poverty of your spirit, and resolve to "go forth and sin no more."

Spiritual Poverty of St. Joseph

What can be said about the spiritual poverty of St. Joseph that hasn't already been revealed through Scripture? You're probably thinking that you don't remember a single word spoken by St. Joseph in Scripture, and you'd be correct. His silence is key in understanding his spiritual poverty. If he was the spouse of a sinless woman and the foster father of the Son of God, then what could he say that would be greater than what either of them said? Nothing, but his actions and obedience to God were the fruits of his spiritual poverty.

If you ponder St. Joseph and his simplicity, you may think that it means that everything should be reduced to the absolute minimum: all of your possessions should be minimized, food should be reduced to the basics, and so on. This belief does a great disservice to the virtue of simplicity (a key component of this beatitude). Minimalism is an incomplete and inadequate understanding of simplicity. Simplicity, in a sense, is a facet of meekness (but we'll get to that in another chapter).

Just as Jesus is meek, St. Joseph chose the best balance of work and life to become a simple man. Simplicity is the intersection of thought, obedience, and action. St. Joseph was obedient to God by his great care and thoughtfulness toward wholeheartedly protecting and providing for Jesus and Mary. Instead of pursuing wealth, he worked enough to support the family but without excess or extravagance. He had purpose to his simplicity, and this purpose is where we, as parents, should be focusing our attention (along with our prayers for intercession from St. Joseph).

Work on being simple so that you have purpose to your actions that are tempered with obedience to God and thoughtfulness of your family. It's a tall order, but since being a parent is a lifelong pursuit, be kind to yourself throughout this process. There will be many days in which you pick yourself up, dust yourself off, and groan with disappointment. I'm sure St. Joseph had days like that in his workshop, so he will certainly feel compassion for the rough road you're treading upon.

Bringing Poverty of Spirit Into Habit and Home

As mentioned earlier, our culture tends to equate simplicity, or poverty of spirit, with the concept of minimalism. Societal minimalism, while good on a basic level, falls short of fostering the motives behind living with less or doing without. For example, many modern minimalists pride themselves on owning, say, no more than fifty items total or living in a home that is less than a thousand square feet.

On a practical level for Catholics who may have larger families, living in a small space and only owning fifty items doesn't really make sense. We have to look a bit deeper into our lifestyle and see what can reasonably be shifted or eliminated so that we can live this beatitude more fully.

Some of us live on two incomes, others on one. Some of us have one child, others nine. What may be feasible for one family does not work for another. Therefore, these are very open-ended and general suggestions for how you can incorporate poverty of spirit into new habits and welcome them in your daily home life.

First, try to evaluate what your income is and what you spend. Budgeting can be tedious, but it's an important first step. In our family, we reconfigure our budget on an annual basis and hang up every single outgoing expense, as well as what we are planning to save, on a simple spreadsheet in our office. It really helps bring perspective and balance to what our priorities are, as well as what we need to change, with our habits of spending.

For example, I (Jeannie) was a shoe fanatic when Ben and I first got married. I boasted a collection of over fifty pairs in every funky and flashy variety you could imagine. But slowly, over time, I saw the excessive spending and inordinate attachment to my shoe collection. And I started paring down what I owned until, last year, I was able to get a good, solid collection of six pairs that included practical and professional options (snow boots, hiking sandals, sneakers, flats, etc.).

While Jeannie focused on clothes and shoes, I (Ben) was into building firearms. It was an expensive hobby, but a habit I could initially afford. After we had been married several years, I realized how much time and money was going into building guns, and I started to sell my collection—reluctantly at first, but I gradually developed an honest intention to shift my attention from hobbies to prayer and family life.

When considering what "stuff" in your home to get rid of, stick to the 75 percent rule: of everything you own, get rid of 75 percent in each category: shoes, clothing, toys, books, housewares, DVDs, etc. Make it a point to go through closets on a regular basis. The job will seem less overwhelming if you commit to cleaning out one room per month and make it a family affair! Select three piles: keep, toss, donate. (And what you donate should be in good condition.)

Finally, be firm in your resolve not to buy more things to replace what you've purged. Live with less, but do so in the spirit of evangelical poverty, knowing that your lifestyle will be simpler and less complicated. You won't have as much to clean, find, keep track of, repair, etc. In turn, you can focus, both individually and as a family, on ways you can volunteer your time to help those who are marginalized or impoverished.

Being poor in spirit can look very different for each family. It requires an ongoing examination of one's attitude and attachment toward money, material goods, social status, and appearance. We must all keep in mind that daily prayer as a family, disciplined quiet time for personal reflection, and frequent confession will contribute to rooting out any vices that contribute to a superfluous or extravagant lifestyle. This beatitude involves lifelong conversion and intentional generosity.

Action Plan

Toddlers and Preschoolers

Take your child on a nature walk. Have her look at all the varieties of flowers and trees, birds and animals. Listen to the evensong of the birds at night, and go stargazing in the summer. Catch some fireflies. As you do, ask your child who made all of these wondrous delights. Explain that God loves us so much that he gave us all of the colors and varieties of foods, plants, and animals to enjoy.

Elementary Age

Act out the creation story using homemade costumes and props. Practice lines using the book of Genesis. Once everything is in order, select an evening to invite grandparents or godparents over for some popcorn to enjoy the show. Use the story as a way to educate your child about the miracles surrounding him every day, while also teaching him to be grateful for such gifts from God. Bonus—have a discussion afterward!

Adolescence

Have your child pick a saint that interests her, and invite her to research a bit more about the life of this saint. Discuss what attributes of this saint's life and character really strike your child. Ask what she thinks it means to be poor in spirit, and probe a bit further into how she might be able to grow in this beatitude at home, at school, on her team, at her job, or in youth group. (Hint: You can use the saint profile below to get started!)

Saint Profile: Blessed Solanus Casey, OFM Capuchin

Blessed Solanus Casey was born the sixth of sixteen children to Irish immigrants in the late nineteenth century. Although he was in love twice, neither relationship evolved into marriage, which led Solanus to question whether he may have had a vocation to the religious life. Knowing how much a religious vocation would delight his parents, who longed for a son of theirs to become a priest, Solanus investigated one particular order—the Capuchins.

The Capuchins, or Order of Francis Minor (OFM), is a particular communal branch of Franciscans, and Solanus knew about them from his brother Edward, who considered applying to become a Capuchin. Solanus struggled with his academics immensely, and because of this, he was nearly dismissed by the order. Yet a few of the Capuchins who met Solanus saw incredible virtue in him and decided to give him a chance.

Once Solanus began his studies in seminary, he struggled, once again, to pass language courses. His poor grades earned him very degrading nicknames among the other seminarians, and even among some of the ordained brothers and priests, but Solanus said nothing and took it all with unwavering interior peace. He believed that even the ridicules he endured were gifts from God and so accepted them with serene resignation.

Solanus was ordained, but barely. His superiors decided to make him a limited priest, which meant he could not absolve anyone in confession, nor could he preach homilies. Again, Father Solanus accepted this without question as part of God's plan for his life.

Eventually, Father Solanus was assigned very menial tasks in the St. Bonaventure Friary—cleaning toilets, sweeping floors, kitchen duty, and ultimately, answering the door as a porter. People who knew Father Solanus were astounded by his remarkable joy and the optimistic attitude he maintained throughout these uncomely jobs he was required to perform out of obedience. But the one job that earned Father Solanus the title "Venerable" was that of doorkeeper.

As unpretentious as he was, Father Solanus eventually became well known for his spiritual charisms of healing and prophecy. As lay visitors would flock to the friary only to speak with Father Solanus briefly or perhaps receive a quick blessing from him, many would return to their communities and report miraculous healings after seeing Father Solanus. Once the word spread, the friary doors were congested every day with visitors who insisted they see Father Solanus.

Naturally, he spoke with everyone who came to see him, but this popularity was not an issue of pride for him. He always attributed their spiritual conversions and healings to Masses that were said on behalf of his devotees. Often, Father Solanus would give his visitors an unofficial penance, which usually included enrolling themselves or the holy souls in purgatory in the Seraphic Mass Association.

Over time, his superiors caught on to the crowds who admired Father Solanus, so he was required to keep record of every person who reported miraculous healings or con- versions. Obediently, Father Solanus did this, and thousands of miracles were reported—through his own hand—which most of his modern devotees attribute to his intercession.

Fr. Solanus Casey epitomized the virtue of poverty of spirit. He owned nothing and lived an incredibly simple life—sim- ple academically and simple in childlike faith. His emptiness of spirit was precisely why God chose to use Solanus as an instrument of hope to people who had lost their faith or had been doomed with irreversible medical prognoses.

Toward the end of his life, one of his Capuchin brothers noticed that Father Solanus's gait was becoming slower and seemingly more painful. When this Capuchin took a look at

Father Solanus's legs, they were so raw from cancer that they almost appeared as flesh falling off bone. The brother asked Father Solanus, "Where does it hurt, Solanus?" And Solanus replied, "It hurts all over, thanks be to God. *Deo gratias!*"

The last words of Father Solanus Casey were, "I give my soul to Jesus Christ." What an example we have as parents—and what an intercessor—of poverty of spirit, or humility. When we are tempted to yell at our children because we presume we are right; when we are irritated or impatient; when we think we have all the answers to our children's problems and crises, we can turn to Blessed Solanus and ask his intercession to make us humble—as he was—and to turn to God in this act of self-abnegation so that we may reach our children with love and mercy.

Prayer

Heavenly Father, you gave me the great task of raising these souls to one day be with you in heaven for all eternity. Sometimes I think I know what my child should do, but my words become garbled cacophony when I speak out of pride rather than from the heart. So teach me, Father, to talk to my children with the heart language of a simple and childlike spirit, knowing that I must model for them what it means to be grateful for what we have rather than seeking to acquire more or coveting what isn't mine to take. Teach me to be poor in spirit and to live in poverty of spirit so that my children will practice generous giving rather than selfish living. Amen.

CHAPTER 2

Blessed Are They Who Mourn, for They Will Be Comforted

The source of all true consolation is found in the mystery of the Lord's Passion. Divine consolation does not come only to put an end to suffering . . . rather, it is something born out of suffering.

—Father Jacques Philippe[2]

Jeannie

Baby showers are filled with blissful and joyful gifts, advice, and games. I remember my first pregnancy with Felicity and how naïve I was about motherhood, especially at my baby shower. No one ever told me about the scary stuff that often happens, and for good reason—who wants to frighten a new mommy-to-be when she is carrying the miracle of human life within her? Yet, in a way, I felt duped once Felicity was born, because suddenly everything was new, different, and yes, terrifying. I found myself frozen with

---

2   Jacques Philippe, *The Eight Doors to the Kingdom*, 86.

fear, because no one prepared me for the reality of childbirth and the pain of postpartum blues.

Once Sarah came along, an entirely new level of scary emerged as Ben and I desperately tried to remedy our fears by educating ourselves about her rare disease and determining whether she would live for very long. Of course, statistics don't suffice when it comes to parenthood, and there is no universal manual for moms and dads.

The fact is we will mourn as mothers. Some of us mourn over the changes we experience in our bodies as we feel every ache and movement of pregnancy, childbirth, and postpartum hormonal letdown. Postpartum depression is also very real and should be treated when moms feel overwhelmed, incapable, paralyzed with fear, or contemplating suicide.

Even more, we understand more fully what Our Lady felt as she watched her Son endure unfathomable torture and die an excruciating death right before her eyes. We, too, will know that helpless feeling as our children grow up and discover betrayal from friends, heartbreak from a boyfriend or girlfriend, physical pain after a surgery, or even struggles with mental illness, autism, learning disabilities, bullying, and a myriad of other trials that are certain to come their way.

We learn early on as moms that our children must suffer, and we suffer alongside them. Though all of us would rather go through the mental and physical anguish for our children than watch them sob, scream, or seclude themselves, we realize that we cannot prevent the unforeseen tribulations that will someday come their way. And that's tough to grasp when you are holding a newborn baby, soaking up her coos and babbles, inhaling the scent of her fresh innocence.

We don't want to acknowledge that life will be hard for our children as they grow up. And in that suffering comes the pain of a mother that is only understood when a child struggles.

Shortly after Sarah was born, Ben and I were confronting the inevitable and dreaded surgery that all kids with Apert syndrome must endure—a cranial vault reconstruction. At six months old, Sarah had to have her skull cut open, which would allow her brain room to grow. I didn't want to face this. In fact, I wanted to run as far away as possible. But I knew that God would give me strength if I stayed rather than fled.

Sarah needed her mom more than ever. Though I didn't want to see her head bandaged and bleeding, I knew I had to muster the courage to watch her suffer and still accompany her in that pain. She needed my reassuring voice, my gentle touch, my presence and gaze. All of this brought the image of the Sorrowful Mother to mind, a devotion I hadn't—until that point—given much attention.

When we mourn, we are tempted to believe it is for naught. So it is when we watch our babies scrape their knees, cry after they get a time-out, become deeply hurt when a boy or girl rejects them, and so on. Our tendency is to eradicate immediately the source of suffering in order to prevent our kids from experiencing any sort of pain. Perhaps the reason for this protective instinct is that we don't want to confront our own suffering. It is far too unbearable to observe the ones you love struggling and hurting in front of us.

Patience and Perseverance

This beatitude offers us eternal hope and a promise. We are blessed when we suffer, but why? It seems that, while suffering is certainly not part of God's perfect will, he does permit it. For some of us, it may be as a test of faith or to help us grow in virtue. For others, it may be to draw us nearer to the Sacred Heart of Jesus and appreciate the sacrificial aspect of love through his ultimate offering of self on the cross. No matter, mourning is an opportunity for us to demonstrate and actively teach our children that it has merit and value. In fact, suffering can be a gift if we look at it through the lens of the cross.

That's what I chose to do after my girls were born and have since struggled with various special needs. I realized that I had to teach them about the value of suffering, to help them turn to Jesus when they were sad or angry or frustrated or lonely. Rather than prevent pain in their lives, I chose to help them offer it as an act of love for Jesus and with a particular intention in mind. For example, Felicity has a deep concern for poor, starving children. When she is upset, I remind her to take a deep breath and offer her struggle in union with Jesus for the poor children.

According to St. Thomas Aquinas, patience is also called "long-suffering." Both patience and perseverance are what he considered "sub-virtues" to the cardinal virtue of fortitude. Think about that as a mom or dad: when you are blessed in the suffering of parenthood, you are given countless opportunities to grow in the virtue of fortitude. That means you are called to excel in striving for what is difficult and arduous for the sake of your and your children's souls.

That's an incredible mystery, isn't it? When we watch our children struggle, make countless mistakes, or experience hardship and betrayal, we're given a holy invitation to grow in fortitude. This virtue is what gives us strength to keep praying for a wayward child, to advocate for a son or daughter with special needs, and never to give up on the eternal salvation of every soul entrusted to us.

Our Lady's Example of Suffering Well

When I think of mourning and the Blessed Mother, I think of Our Lady of Sorrows. Through this title, Mary reminds us as mothers that our suffering is not lost upon God and that God does not waste anything. The specific example pertaining to mourning is the third Mystery of the Seven Sorrows of Mary devotion: the loss of the Child Jesus in the Temple.

Imagine you were in her shoes. She and St. Joseph were part of a caravan that had been traveling away from Jerusalem for an entire day. Can you possibly fathom leaving your child behind for a whole day and spending three additional days looking for him? Most of us would panic at best, maybe hyperventilate or have a nervous breakdown. But not Mary. She was steadfast and strong in her unwavering trust in the Lord. She knew the Father was with her and with Jesus and that she would find him.

Even so, it must have been an incredible heartbreak to be separated from her Son in such a way. Her calm in the midst of uncertainty is a sure example that we, as mothers, must not fret when our children exhibit patterns of behavior that are questionable or even sinful. Even more, if our older children are showing signs of disinterest or even rebellion against the Faith, we can turn to Our Lady of Sorrows and ask her to grant us a share in the perfect peace and trust she displayed when she lost Jesus for a time.

Suffering is not easy, there's no way around that. But in our mourning, the Lord promises his comfort. We may not always feel competent and certainly will make mistakes, but if we turn to the Lord in faith, we can ask him to strengthen our resolve as role models of redemptive suffering. Teaching our children to suffer well by "offering it up" can also add a layer of understanding and endurance when they must struggle with an internal or physical problem.

Even if the ultimate consolation occurs in the afterlife for us, we have everlasting hope in that promise of heaven. Let us strive for heaven and remember to diligently bring our children with us on that path, be it strewn with rocks and thorns or roses and meadows.

Ben

I still remember it as if it were yesterday, even though it was over twenty years ago. I was in high school, and the morning I woke up in September seemed like any other morning. As I came into the kitchen, my dad was standing there, which was never out of the ordinary. I said, "Good morning" in my teenage fog, which was met with these words: "Your grandpa passed away this morning." I felt my blood run ice cold and nothing but numbness wash over me. I was devastated and became riddled with guilt—guilt because my mom had asked me the Sunday before if I wanted to see my grandpa. I had said no with a lame excuse as to why I would delay seeing him until another time. That other time never came.

As a sixteen-year-old, learning of my grandfather's death was a horrifically hard experience, since I had, up to that point, not experienced the death of a close relative. Being young and naïve, I didn't carry the sense of mortality that I have today, especially since many of my encounters with death as an adult have been from my experience as a law enforcement officer. Not only was dealing with my grandpa's death hard, but the manner in which the news was delivered was also troublesome.

I don't fault my father or my family for delivering the bad news so abruptly; I can only conclude that my dad was used to receiving bad news in the same way, since his father was a World War II veteran and too often must have received abrupt news of the deaths of his friends and fellow soldiers. What would have been most helpful to me, though, would have been my parents helping me to work through the initial shock of this news.

This was the grandpa with whom I had spent so much time fishing, watching the old Tom & Jerry cartoon, and eating ice cream. (Grandparents are always good for getting sweets, as most kids quickly find out.) I felt as if I had let him down by not being there for him in his final days. The lesson I quickly learned was that we never know how many days any of us has left. When someone's health is failing, it should certainly be a time to not only practice the Works of Mercy but also remind ourselves that our time on earth is short.

In this state of guilt, sadness, and mourning over the loss of my grandfather, there was a moment during the eulogy at his funeral that made me smile and gave me a glimpse of comfort. My maternal grandparents were both aviators and taught fighter pilots during World War II. They both loved anything that had to do with aviation until the day they died. During the funeral, everyone in attendance could hear an airplane flying close by.

The plane then made the unmistakable sound of doing a loop in the air. Even the priest who was giving the eulogy said, "Well, that loop by the plane was for your grandfather." It brought a smile to my face and everyone else who was in attendance that day. In my state of mourning, I felt the consolation of what may have appeared to be a random event, but we smiled, believing it was a sign of God's providence.

This sense of mourning, blessed with a moment of comfort, has taught me a lesson in perseverance: to persevere through dryness in relationships, life circumstances, and prayer. Helping our children through the dryness of mourning with persistence can pay off for them in the future.

Our oldest daughter, Felicity, has felt this sense of mourning and dryness from the perspective of feeling like a "forgotten child" because of the attention that has been put on her sister's medical care. We spend so much time and effort with phone calls, doctor's appointments, and other related issues that she often feels left out and forgotten. (I shall digress for one moment and just say, for the record, that my wife does the lion's share of the phone calls and regular doctor's appointments. She most certainly deserves the credit for all that hard work.) In any case, Felicity mourns the loss of attention and focus that she craves and sees her sister getting. This sadness has become a struggle for her and for us as her parents, to balance out the attention that our three children receive.

As parents, we want to bring comfort to our children, but we must help our children realize that we, as parents, can only offer *temporal* comfort, while God provides *eternal* comfort. We certainly shouldn't sugarcoat the truth about suffering and loss, but when our children are aware that their eternal reward awaits, despite the inevitable road of difficulty, we set them up to persevere and trust in God when mourning sets in.

In order to help my children in the future with understanding and accepting suffering, there are two main concepts that I need to help them balance. The first is the acceptance of the reality of a situation. In the example I provided earlier, I had to accept the death of my grandfather. Secondly, there needs to be a follow-up to the pain of the situation. Not only should the reality be accepted, but the pain must be acknowledged too.

Once my children feel safe in accepting the reality and expressing the pain of the situation, then the healing can begin. If we deny the reality of suffering and ignore the pain, then we are left with a festering wound that can linger for years. In order to give my children the tenacity that they need to live in this world, I need to be comfortable with their discomfort and allow them to cry or be angry. Facing stark realities must be tempered with the hope and healing of Jesus, and leading my family to this understanding is a large part of my primary vocation as a father to three girls.

St. Joseph's Patience

Fathers don't spend a lot of time being heard. There's a constant push for our voice to be at the forefront of all the decisions in the household, as well as at work. The fact that St. Joseph did not utter one spoken word in all of Scripture should give us pause as we consider the first two sentences.

Think about the patience it must require to have perfect interior peace; instead of words, we let our actions speak. St. Joseph did many things that are written in Scripture, but there is no record of his words. I'm sure that he mourned internally at the loss of many things but bore them without complaint and in perfect obedience to God's will. Once again, it was with action and not words that he took on the difficulties surrounding him.

So often our own peace is easily disturbed and is followed by griping and a stream of words that express our lamentations. We waste the time for action by filling the space around us with complaints and rants. I know, because I am certainly guilty of this. Maybe instead, we should pause and come to grips with the reality of the situation and put that hurt or complaint to prayer and, dare I say, *praise* God for the difficulties.

We may mourn the loss of a child to a life of dissipation, or the hardship of caring for an aging parent or child with a disability, but these situations of mourning should turn us more towards *action in prayer* than *words of complaint*. The very difficulties we are bearing could be our stepping stones to heaven, if only we would take that leap of faith to the next level of trusting God.

Without a doubt, patience plays in trust as well. What we suffer may go on for a very long time, and that is where we must have fortitude. As fathers, the suffering that we bear ourselves or when we must watch others suffer is the grand battle in which we must participate in order to be strengthened for the next world. Strengthening our souls through trials is the ultimate training in becoming patient and in learning to act on God's prompting for trust and prayer. In these battles, St. Joseph is there with us to be the reflection of patience, as he helps us turn our laments into actions of prayer and resignation to God's will.

Mourning any sort of loss will always be hard for us to express as fathers, but crying, praying, or meditating on uniting our suffering with Christ will never be meritless. While nothing was mentioned in Scripture about Jesus and the loss of his adoptive father, St. Joseph, it would be wise for all of us as fathers to ponder this loss. Meditate on the pain in Jesus's heart for having lost such an important person who was present his whole life, who modeled deeds, if not words, in all things.

Let St. Joseph's actions guide us on our own journeys as fathers, both from the perspective of Jesus in losing St. Joseph and from the patience and humility of St. Joseph. He knew that he could never be perfect as Jesus is, yet he did everything possible to be a model father. We, too, are guaranteed to lose our earthly fathers in this life. Our losses may come with tears, but we know that the bitterness we taste now will be infinitely sweeter in heaven.

Bringing Mourning Into Habit and Home

It's not exactly desirable to *bring* suffering into our home, is it? Certainly suffering was never part of God's original plan for humankind, but it entered through the first sin, as we well know. If we truly believe that God doesn't waste anything, including suffering, then as a Resurrection people, we have to admit that suffering can be a *gift*.

As parents, we never want our children to suffer. Sometimes we take painstaking measures to shield and shelter our kids from the inevitable struggles they will face as they grow up. But perhaps this beatitude can direct us in another way: to understand how our suffering and the struggles of our children can bring us closer to each other and, ultimately, closer to God.

Father Jacques Philippe, in his book *The Eight Doors to the Kingdom: Meditations on the Beatitudes*, offers this particular insight about the hidden blessing in our mourning: "Experiencing difficulty equips us to understand and comfort others in their difficulties."[3] We can thus determine that suffering strengthens us for a deeper purpose: to accompany others who are in the midst of pain and sorrow.

When Sarah was born, we didn't have anyone to talk to who understood Apert syndrome. There was a deep chasm of loneliness that seemed to separate us from our friends and family, despite efforts on both ends to find common ground.

---

[3]   Ibid., 94.

Apert syndrome was the giant elephant we all couldn't ignore; we suffered a terrible time of mourning the struggles we had to undergo with Sarah's diagnosis.

Only recently did we learn what this gift of accompaniment in times of sorrow could be. I (Jeannie) have a friend from grade school, whom I ran into at an obstetric appointment when I was pregnant with Veronica. We chatted in the waiting room for a few minutes and then parted ways once we were called back to the exam room.

A few short weeks later, I received a message on social media from my friend. She shared an incredible story with me. After she had given birth to her son, she and her husband were leaving the hospital when they passed an Amish gentleman who congratulated them on their new bundle. My friend saw he was wearing a nametag that said, "New Father," so she also congratulated him.

He briefly paused, then spoke. "I'm not sure what to do. We just found out our newborn son has something called Apert syndrome." Immediately, my friend thought of me and the conversation we'd had only weeks prior. She contacted me to ask if I would mind talking with this family and helping them make sense out of this new journey. Of course, I cheerfully agreed!

After giving the Amish family our phone number, the father called me while he and his wife were still in the hospital, trying to wrap their minds around the diagnosis and what their son's life would entail. As I answered their questions, I could sense their fear and uncertainty. Instantly, I remembered five years before when Ben and I were in the same situation—with no one to help us answer our questions.

What a gift to be able to offer comfort and encouragement to this family! After speaking on the phone, we agreed to stay in touch and meet one day. I mailed the family a small packet I typed with information about helpful physicians, therapies, non-profits, etc. that have significantly eased the burden of caring for a child with a rare disease for us.

This is what the gift of accompaniment looks like when we walk with others who are suffering. As parents, we set the example for our children to understand how important and necessary it is for us to do what we are called to do when we encounter other families who are in need of something we can offer them. Reaching out in this way is a powerful way to incorporate the practice of the Works of Mercy in your family.

A final thought: 2 Corinthians 1:3–4 reads, "Blessed be the God and Father of our Lord Jesus Christ, the Father of compassion and God of all encouragement, who encourages us in our every affliction, so that we may be able to encourage those who are in any affliction with the encouragement with which we ourselves are encouraged by God." Some translations use the word "comfort" in place of "encouragement." Think about that for a moment and read the passage again with the word "comfort."

When we live this beatitude fully, we understand that we are called to bring comfort and encouragement to others who are in need of consolation, bringing Christ's healing balm to wounded and weary hearts. That's the hidden beauty of suffering and the gift it brings to a hurting world.

Action Plan

Toddlers and Preschoolers

Learning about suffering can be tough, more so for parents than for their kids. Even small children are surprisingly resilient and grasp more than we realize about hardship. For ages three through preschool age, doing crafts and reading books to explain life, death, and the afterlife work really well. For instance, if you choose to do a paper craft, such as constructing a butterfly with different colored paper, you can explain the process of a caterpillar becoming a butterfly and how it must "die" before it can be "resurrected." There are also countless examples of children's books about various aspects of grief and suffering if you search online.

Elementary Age

Older kids may benefit from creating a memorial album as part of an overview of suffering and mourning. The album can include photos, collages, favorite phrases, or quotations from Scripture or the saints, etc. At this age, kids should definitely begin to understand the concept of "offering it up," or handing Jesus their pain, whether emotional or physical, in order to benefit someone else who is suffering.

Adolescence

It's often difficult for parents to encourage their teens to open up about difficult emotions, but there are healthy outlets you can suggest that will still make your teen feel as if he or she is able to maintain some semblance of privacy. One way is to give them a journal and explain that they can write down their feelings, draw or sketch, pen prayers to God, etc. This is their private space to share what's on their hearts. Explaining the concept of redemptive suffering more deeply will also benefit your teen, even if he or she doesn't openly say that it helps.

Saint Profile: St. Elizabeth Ann Seton

St. Elizabeth Ann Seton, though most well known for her influence in founding the first Catholic girls' school in the United States, was no stranger to loss and mourning. Born to a prominent Episcopalian family, Elizabeth eventually converted to Catholicism, which was the first test (of many) in how she would handle the sense of being forsaken, lonely, and persecuted. Many of her family and friends openly chastised her for her conversion. Nevertheless, she persevered through this trial and remained steadfast in her decision to follow the Catholic Church.

When Elizabeth was only three years old, her mother died, leaving her with a deep emotional chasm. Her father remarried and had five additional children with Elizabeth's stepmother, but Elizabeth was never fully accepted or loved by her stepmother. After Elizabeth's father and stepmother separated later in life, she was further ostracized by both family and friends. Again, the theme of loss and mourning reemerged as Elizabeth desperately attempted to make sense of losing two mothers in very different ways.

Eventually Elizabeth's husband, William, died at a fairly young age from ongoing complications of tuberculosis, leaving Elizabeth a widow with small children. She and William were very close, so his death was a deep loss and source of emotional and spiritual pain for her. Perhaps this time of life was her second experience in what we might call "spiritual darkness," as she mourned the loss of her beloved life's companion. Again, she remained faithful to the call toward conversion to Catholicism and continued her faith journey with heartfelt and fervent prayer, trusting in God's providence.

As if these losses weren't devastating enough, Elizabeth's sons also died at a young age. It was after their deaths that she, along with her daughters, decided to found the Sisters of Charity religious order. Throughout the sorrow she endured, Elizabeth maintained her devotion to Our Lady, the Eucharist, and reading Scripture. Perhaps these devotions provided the necessary grace and consolation she needed to regain strength after each death she grieved.

St. Elizabeth Ann Seton, therefore, is a fine example of one who overcame many types of grief in her life, including literal death, but also death of her wealthy lifestyle, death of some of her relationships, even death to herself. She teaches us as parents, as well as providing a strong witness to our children, that suffering can be lived with *joy*. Within each loss, Elizabeth struggled to be sure, but she endured by being faithful to God and remaining rooted in the sacraments. Because of this, her legacy will never be forgotten.

Prayer

Heavenly Father, I don't often suffer well. Sometimes I want to run away from life's struggles, whether big or small. Yet I know that you call me to something more in my hardships. You ask me to carry my cross daily and follow you. Help me, by your grace, to accept my sufferings with confidence in your love and mercy so that I might assist my children to know how beautiful it is to sacrifice one's comforts for the sake of souls. Amen.

Chapter 3

Blessed Are the Meek, for They Will Inherit the Land

*The meek are those who know how to suffer
their neighbor and themselves.*

—Father Jacques Philippe[4]

Jeannie

Becoming meek involves the foundation of humility. A person cannot become gentle and kind without first submitting him- or herself to obedience to God in all things, especially during times of trial and tribulation. St. Gregory of Nyssa believed that each beatitude built upon its predecessor, subsequently revealing a deeper life of virtue expressed more fully. Meekness, along with humility, are certainly not popular virtues for which to aspire in our modern day. I recall wrestling with this virtue at a young age.

---

4   Jacques Philippe, *The Eight Doors to the Kingdom*, 118.

When I was about five years old, I spent quite a bit of time in my bedroom, usually contemplating or imagining lofty ideals that included Jesus, Mary, the saints, and the afterlife. But I could not relate to Mary as she was portrayed to me in religion class. She, being the epitome of meekness, seemed to me a woman beyond my understanding.

As I tried to pray to Our Lady, I often felt rising shame and guilt accompany and even thwart my prayers. It wasn't clear to me until I was much older that these feelings were caused by my sense of inadequacy because I was opinionated, feisty, and prone to fits of anger. I felt ashamed of myself in the face of such humility and gentleness, so Mary's meekness was something I believed I could never attain in this life.

Recently, I shared this experience with one of my friends. Her response was profound. She reminded me that, although the Blessed Mother was most certainly meek and gentle, she also epitomized the virtues I naturally possessed—zeal, perseverance, and hope. She perfects every virtue, not just meekness. There is, after all, something we all can relate to about Mary's personal and virtuous attributes.

Now that I am a mother, I see the importance of growing in this virtue—and of frequently turning to Our Lady for help. Though I'm still prone to impatience and yelling, I've grown in perhaps small, but measurable, ways as a parent by practicing the beatitude of becoming meek. I do this when I stay calm instead of losing my cool (which has happened on occasion). I practice meekness when I pray before responding to my children.

But I think what helps me to respond to my daughters with compassion rather than fury is when I take time to see a situation through their little eyes. It's easy to blow up at a three-year-old who decides that throwing a major tantrum is the perfect response to not getting ice cream for dessert, but if I take a deep breath and utter a quick prayer heavenward, it changes things drastically.

Somehow that tantrum, though intolerable, makes sense to me when I realize the emotional immaturity of my three-year-old. I also consider extraneous variables that may have contributed to the tantrum—no nap, a long car ride, feeling hungry, etc. It's not that Sarah receives no discipline for her tantrum, because she does. But the discipline is done in love rather than anger, and that makes all the difference.

I've noticed when I preface a consequence with a soft voice to my girls, while hugging them and telling them I understand they are angry (tired, hungry, bored, etc.), that gesture of kindness—meekness—changes the way they listen and respond to the consequence of their behavior. Sure, there might still be some sort of rebuttal, but most of the time, they realize why they need to be corrected and how it's good for them to learn what is right and what is wrong.

I think it's tough for most of us to find that perfect balance between mercy and justice when it comes to responding to our children. At times, there seems to be more one than the other, and then we may feel guilty or ashamed that we didn't discipline consistently or perhaps that we did discipline, but there was no compassion, no mercy involved.

But returning to this beatitude when we are tempted to explode or lose patience with our little ones (and even teens) can remind us of how magnanimous it is to be meek and kind. In fact, we are told that we will "inherit the land," obviously not literally, but in a figurative sense. We are essentially bringing about God's kingdom on earth when we demonstrate meekness, especially to our children.

Our Lady's Perfect Humility

Let's return to Our Lady of Sorrows and ponder for a moment the second Mystery of the Seven Sorrows, which is the Flight into Egypt. I've thought a lot about what might have transpired when the Holy Family was peacefully slumbering and then suddenly awakened by St. Joseph, who urgently told the Blessed Mother to rise and get ready to leave. I'm definitely a mom who needs her sleep. If Ben woke me up in the middle of the night and said we were leaving, I know I would have a million questions and would probably protest.

But Our Lady did just the opposite: she quietly and obediently gathered what few things they possessed, nestled Jesus against her, and followed her husband. She did this for a couple of reasons, I think. One is that she knew God had ordained St. Joseph to be the head of the family. Because of this, she also knew God was leading St. Joseph's heart to protect both her and Jesus. The other is that she was perfectly humble, which is what motivated her obedience to St. Joseph and, essentially, to God.

As mothers, we are called to do the same. It's tough, but this beatitude asks that we grow in tenderness, sensitivity, and humility. Meekness is the virtue that opens our hearts to grace. Father Jacques Philippe says that "meekness is . . . the characteristic attribute of the Holy Spirit's action."[5] In other

---

[5]   Ibid., 102–3.

words, we have to be receptive to the movements of the Holy Spirit, however odd or inopportune they may seem.

Sometimes that means following our husband's bizarre intuitions. I did this when Sarah was about two years old. I was on the leadership team of a women's retreat at our parish, and another woman on our team had approached me with what seemed like fantastic news: she wanted to help organize a fundraiser to raise money for Sarah's ongoing medical care!

We exchanged phone numbers and agreed to follow up within a week of the initial conversation. She worked as a sous chef in a high-end Chicago restaurant and said the owner of the hotel where the restaurant was located had already agreed to donate a Chicago getaway package that we could raffle, with full proceeds benefiting Sarah's medical bills.

It seemed too good to be true, but I trusted her. After I approached Ben with the idea, he agreed to meet with her at our house and hash out the details. She came to our house highly disorganized and ill-prepared, but I brushed it off and gave her the benefit of the doubt. Ben, however, was much more skeptical than I was. In fact, he became suspicious.

After she left, Ben had a nagging feeling he couldn't shake. I was walking on the hope that this opportunity would help relieve some of the creeping financial burden we'd been accruing. Because Ben was a reserve sheriff's deputy at the time, he saw some red flags in our conversation with this woman and did some of his own sleuthing. As a result, he discovered this woman had a long history of fraud in her criminal history!

What I learned was to trust Ben's leadership in our family. Like the Blessed Mother with St. Joseph, I chose to step aside and allow God's grace to work through the authority he granted Ben by divine law. This instance was one of several times where I had absolutely no inkling of imminent spiritual or physical danger on our family, while Ben most certainly did. If I had usurped his authority, our family would have suffered terribly.

Being meek as a woman means submitting yourself to the authority God has placed above you. It means relinquishing the need to have the final say, to always be right, to demand what honestly doesn't belong to you. This submission can be incredibly difficult, but that is why the virtue of humility is so central to becoming meek. Humility debases the need for power and prestige. It calms the soul so that you are more able to see things clearly in the spirit of gentleness rather than anger or pride.

Ben

Until recently I've always had a skewed perspective of what meekness truly is. For some strange reason, I was always under the impression that meekness was the "go along to get along" attitude that went along with obedience. Was I ever wrong about this! I think to a degree that misperception has stunted my spiritual growth. Thankfully, this misperception has been corrected, and I'm a better man for it. For a moment, let's explore the idea of meekness and how that applies to us as men and fathers.

When our children misbehave and warrant discipline, we, as men, have the strength to plant a pretty solid swat on the rear ends of our darling children. To swat their posterior with the force you would reserve for a full-grown adult would certainly be cruel and not warranted for the situation. By controlling the strength you have and metering it appropriately to the situation, you have just exercised meekness. Meekness can be a wonderful virtue for men because it engages our minds to try to be more Christlike, in the sense that we have the strength or ability to do something but we are temperate enough in our response so as to be just and not cruel. This meekness does not only apply to physical actions but also to our speech and attitudes.

When looking at the meekness of Christ, then, we can certainly learn some lessons. Not only was he fully man, but he was fully God as well. If he had wanted to, he could have easily vaporized the entire Roman Empire with lightning, a pillar of fire, or any other means he would have wanted to use, but he chose not to. This point may be a little extreme, but it drives home the concept that, as God, he could do anything, but because of his meekness and love for all of us, he gave us the choice to love and follow him or reject him. There was no coercion or force involved, and his example and words were left for us enshrined in the Scriptures.

Just as Jesus has shown us, our meekness as fathers should be demonstrated to our children. Since Jesus sacrificed his life for his bride, the Church, so should we sacrifice for our brides as an example to our children. In our meekness of service to our family, we should sacrifice plainly but without boasting or complaint. This can be a tall order since we, myself included, can be pretty good at complaining at times.

Would it be nice to go out and get that nice new truck instead of a minivan for the family? Sure, it would! You can imagine blasting through the snow or mud in four-wheel drive, but reality creeps in, and the only thing you'll be blasting through is the parking lot of the local grocery store to pick up My Little Pony band-aids for your daughter's skinned knee. Did I mention that meekness has a component of humility? If your pride feels bruised, then you've quickly realized this truth.

Meekness can show up in many different situations and is comprised of different virtues. One lesson I've learned in meekness as it pertains to charity was an example from our oldest daughter. For her sixth birthday, she stated that she wanted only a couple of rather small items but that she wanted everyone to bring a donation of food or money for "the poor children." I can state with authority I had no such lofty ideas when I was turning six. She exhibited the trait of meekness by knowing that she could ask for just about anything but was selfless enough to ask for donations for the poor. Not only did she display true concern for others, but she challenged me as well.

One of my hobbies is collecting and smoking pipes. (Yes, just like your grandpa, and it's a hobby, not a habit.) For the moment, let's look past any feelings you have on tobacco and focus on my daughter's challenge. Near her sixth birthday, she said, "Daddy, you have a lot of pipes. Maybe you should sell one for the poor children." Out of the mouths of babes. So, after some consideration, I chose a pipe and put it up for sale. I could have sold it, bought another, and further buried myself in my hobby, but with the sincere challenge from my daughter, I got a lesson in being meek.

From this lesson, I now have a greater appreciation of meekness, not only *from* my family, but also as a continued example *for* my family. The more I display this virtue, the more my children will pick up on what I'm doing. It also gets just a little bit easier every time I sacrifice something small, and it's great in building good habits as a parent.

Don't feel you have to show meekness in a big way with your children. If you become overly complex in your thought process, you suddenly have taken away the chance for your kids to learn outside of what's familiar and comfortable for them. You also may think that the task is too large and give up before you've even begun.

Take very small steps and literally *become childlike* so that your kids can process the behaviors they are seeing from you. Sacrifice small things, knowing that you *can* give up that last piece of cake or the extra plate of food for a purpose. As your children watch that you have the capability to do or take more, but refrain to do so out of deference to others, they will begin to process this beatitude of meekness at an early age and carry it throughout their lives.

The Humility of St. Joseph

As fathers, how many times do we associate meekness with weakness? I'm certainly guilty of this, but a talk from one of our parish priests quickly changed my mind on this point. Meekness is certainly not weakness. In fact, it's quite the

opposite. Meekness is having the power to exercise a legitimate strength over someone or something but choosing not
to do so out of mercy and love. Christ is meek because he
most certainly has the power to execute a just sentence of
damnation over all of us, but instead he allows us to tread a
path of mercy and repentance, if we so choose.

St. Joseph was within his rights according to the Mosaic
law to stone Mary because of what seemed to be a child conceived out of wedlock, but he exhibited meekness to its full-
est extent instead. He rejected violence and bloodshed, and
his meekness opened his life and heart to the Holy Spirit,
who gave him the truth of the situation. Once again, St.
Joseph provides a lesson for us in understanding the blessings of being meek. If we exercise meekness, we open our
hearts to the will of God, and he will pour the Holy Spirit
upon us. In turn, the Holy Spirit helps us seek the true good
and the truth in every situation.

We can apply meekness at home when it comes to dealing
with our children, as well as our spouse. Your wife may have
scheduled time with a friend, even though you both discussed earlier that you'd be taking that time to help a friend
or find a quiet moment of down time. It's legitimate to be
upset about that conflict of interests, but meekness means
we can choose to be merciful at the oversight and put the
needs of our spouse before our own.

When it comes to misbehaving children, there can be
a legitimate consequence of losing a favored toy or even a
quick swat on the rear end, and immediately following this
discipline, we can offer an explanation and merciful hug.
These can quickly mend the painful consequence of losing

a toy or privilege. Striving to parallel God's mercy helps us create a road map on how to approach the issues we face in fatherhood.

We should always applaud the truth and help our children understand that telling the truth makes consequences less severe than when they choose to lie. When *we* tell the truth of our sins and shortcomings in Reconciliation, we also model the truth and its impact for the good in our lives. In turn, we hope our children may be truthful to us, and ultimately our heavenly Father, when they witness our attempts to be meek. As we prepare for the sacrament of Reconciliation, we can also prepare our children for their first confession.

Another facet of meekness is compassion, which can be quite difficult for fathers. As our society becomes more self-absorbed and enamored with social media, we lose our ability for empathy and quickly forget the misfortunes of others around us in everyday life. I recently read about compassion in terms of carrying out one of the Corporal Works of Mercy: burying the dead. By being physically close to death, you have compassion for those who bear the suffering of losing a loved one. The reality of this Work of Mercy struck home with me as a former sheriff's deputy who had the unenviable task of moving a dead body from the scene of an accidental overdose, as well as taking pictures of the deceased in a death investigation.

I'm not suggesting that you make your kids physically remove a body or participate in a crime scene photoshoot, but I am suggesting that when they are mature enough to understand death, they can face the difficulties of a funeral with courage or even be a pallbearer. In this brush with death, we learn to have compassion for others and a healthy understanding of our own mortality.

I think frequently of St. Joseph and wonder if he had to help Mary bury her parents or any other family members. Certainly, death was no stranger to the Holy Family, especially for Mary after losing St. Joseph and the eternal sacrifice of her Son. The compassion, meekness, and humility that are all involved in this mortal life can quickly bring us to a greater understanding of death and greater charity towards others.

When we ponder our mortality, we grow in meekness, because we are faced with the reality that we, too, will one day perish in body. Our immortal souls will face their judgment, and we'll be able to look at our life in its entirety—the good, the bad, the ugly. Facing this reality puts into perspective that we cannot live for ourselves alone, but rather for others. Like the example of St. Joseph, who put his needs and wants last of all, we have a greater desire for holiness and virtue as we strive to be meek in both great things and small.

Bringing Meekness Into Habit and Home

How, then, can we teach our kids what it means to be meek? Some concrete ways to do this would be explaining the power of saying "I'm sorry" when we're wrong and "I forgive you" when someone else hurts us. Forgiveness certainly involves meekness. Choosing to be kind, which is an aspect of charity, is another way we can teach our children about this beatitude. For younger children, sharing a beloved toy or allowing a sibling or friend to choose the game to play are ways to be kind. For older children, doing more chores than expected of them might be demonstrations of kindness.

Obedience is really the crux of this beatitude for kids. If we, as parents, are incapable of exhibiting obedience to authority (e.g., all ordained men in the Church, our bosses at work, and ultimately God), how can we expect our children to obey out of a spirit of meekness? One of the things we work on in our home is the concept of "right-away obedience." Initially, our older girls obeyed because they "had to," so they said. It was not out of a sincere desire to do what was right, only to avoid the consequence of punishment.

Over time, they have learned to obey mom and dad out of love for God. Of course, this obedience from love of God isn't *always* the case, but we have to remember that spiritual growth takes time. It's about progress, not perfection, to lift a phrase from Alcoholics Anonymous and Al-Anon. Part of demonstrating meekness is being patient with the mistakes we make as parents and also with the often-messy process of our children developing a true desire to please God.

The point is that we have to return to this beatitude on a daily basis, just as we should return to all of the Beatitudes in some form. Once I (Jeannie) realized that I could still be my brassy, loquacious self and learn to be gentle when the circumstance calls for it, I overcame my shame and began asking Mary to help me grow in humility and meekness. Part of striving for this virtue, then, is for us to forgive ourselves and our children when we inevitably make mistakes. Then we can call upon God to compensate with his grace for where we failed as mom or dad, resting assured that he will provide it abundantly.

Action Plan

Toddlers and Preschoolers

Children, especially young children, aren't naturally meek (typically speaking). Most of their form of pride emerges in tantrums and being selfish with their toys. You can encourage your children to develop this beatitude in a few simple ways. First, teach them how to share out of a sense of generosity rather than duty or obligation. Tell them that sharing is a form of sacrifice and can be offered up to Jesus. Second, share stories about those who are less fortunate and how kindness offered in the form of a smile, a compliment, or a small deed can go a long way to make someone's day. Third, have some form of a sacrifice jar or beads around the house and explain various types of sacrifices (sharing, kind acts, acts of obedience, doing something "extra" without being asked, etc.) and how they can tally up those sacrifices by placing a bead in a jar. At the end of the day or week, the family can see how many gifts were offered to Jesus, and a celebration of some sort incurs.

Elementary Age

At this age, children are witnesses to a plethora of rude comments, bullying, and all sorts of rebellion. Junior-high age especially is rife with relational, social, and physical aggression. Start and continue a conversation with your tween about what's going on with other kids at school or in the neighborhood: "I know a lot of kids your age pick on someone who is different. What do you think about that?" You might be surprised at how your child opens up, more than you expect. Say a prayer to the Holy Spirit and see where he leads the dialogue. The point is to maintain honest and authentic conversations with your child so that he can learn what you value and your expectations on his behavior. For instance, on the topic of ostracizing, you might say, "If you see Jude picking on Jose, what might be a kind gesture to make Jose feel cared for?" This question paves the way for meekness to become a more desired and practiced virtue for your older child.

Adolescence

Learning to be gentle takes time—more for some kids than others. If it is fostered early and often, by the time your child reaches adolescence, it may very well be a virtue that is reinforced rather than explicitly taught. Teens usually find some cause that they care deeply about. Listen to what's important to them and cultivate ways they can show kindness by volunteering for a homeless shelter or spending time with cats or dogs at the animal shelter. Meekness extends to all of God's creation and can include caring for the earth in ways that others may overlook, such as recycling, growing a vegetable garden, and transforming all of these actions into prayers of gratitude and praise to God our Creator.

Saint Profile: St. Alphonsus Liguori

Known as the patron saint of confessors, St. Alphonsus Liguori lived his entire apostolate through the lens of meekness. Born in Italy to nobility, he suffered from poor eyesight and asthma, which complicated his early plans for a military career. Nevertheless, his suffering also granted him the grace to love others with kindness and to enter into their plight through accompaniment.

After a brief stint as a lawyer, Alphonsus felt the call to the priesthood through an interior voice: "Leave the world and give yourself to me." Initially, he entered the Oratory of St. Philip Neri, but his father was opposed to this plan, so Alphonsus agreed to find another path to priesthood and only after he had officially left home. Shortly after leaving home for Naples, he encountered very destitute and abandoned children on the streets, which moved his heart with pity and compassion for them. It was there he ministered to the victims of such poverty and then saw an apparition of the Virgin Mary.

After Our Lady appeared to Alphonsus, he founded the Congregation of the Most Holy Redeemer, mainly because he received confirmation from a nun named Sister Maria Celeste Crostarosa that he was the one God had chosen for the task. The congregation's main apostolate was to minister to impoverished areas, but the priests also combatted a popular heresy at the time: Jansenism.

Because Alphonsus cared deeply for the poor and suffering, he saw Jansenism as a terrible hypocrisy against a merciful God. Jansenists promoted a very strict morality that emphasized original sin and human depravity. The Congregationists believed that people should be treated with mercy rather than as criminals awaiting trial. Alphonsus led them with meekness and never denied absolution to a repentant penitent.

He was eventually appointed bishop and spent his remaining years writing prolifically about the Blessed Mother and the Eucharist, his main loves. Because of a prevailing ailment, he excused himself from the Congregation, retired, and died in the Redemptorist community in Pagani, Italy. The written work that St. Alphonsus left us is evidence of his gentle spirit and compassionate nature.

Prayer

Gentle and gracious God, you came to earth as a tiny child to teach me how to love all of your creation with meekness. Teach me, as a parent, to demonstrate this beatitude to everyone in my life, but most especially to my family. As I pray to grow in meekness, grant me the grace to nurture my children in habits that are kind, gentle, and compassionate so that they may grow into adults who are deeply concerned about others. Amen.

CHAPTER 4

Blessed Are They Who Hunger and Thirst for Righteousness, for They Will Be Satisfied

Justice toward others is the measure of our relationship with God. . . . The thirst for justice is a thirst to let oneself be adjusted to God and to others.

—Father Jacques Philippe[6]

Jeannie

When I think of hunger and thirst, my second grader and kindergartner immediately come to mind: "Mo-om! I'm hungry! I'm really, *really* thirsty!" There's a sense of urgency with deep hunger and thirst, which makes the metaphor very tangible as it pertains to a *spiritual* hunger and thirst.

---

[6]   Jacques Philippe, *The Eight Doors to the Kingdom*, 127.

Remember how Jesus said as he hung on the cross, "I thirst"? Of course, he meant that his palate was excruciatingly dry, as some of us may have experienced from time to time, but he also meant he thirsted for *souls*. His thirst went deeper than the mere corporeal need for water or wine to slake his thirst.

When we hunger and thirst in a spiritual sense, we long for something so much that it cannot be quelled without divine grace. In a sense, we should also thirst the way Jesus did—and does—for souls, most especially for our own soul, our spouse's soul, and the souls of our children. That thirst, then, will be slaked by our prayers and acts of mortification, the small sacrifices we've discussed in previous chapters, and the ways God stirs in us to guide and shape our kids towards heaven.

A hunger and thirst for righteousness, then, means that we pine for justice to be fulfilled—in the world, yes, but also in our family. It means we truly desire for God's will to come to fruition in our hearts and homes.

I remember a strong burning in my heart for justice when I was a child. It was a justice I believed was righteous because I always noticed wrongs happening all around me: bullying at school, kids who lied, adults who didn't keep their promises, and even other injustices, like littering trash (which really bothered me) or hurting animals. When these occurred, my heart was afflicted in a most unusual way, but then I was moved to want to amend the situation—promptly and rightly.

This sense of justice is noble at its root and in its purest form, but rarely do we express anything purely, especially when it is a virtue that has not been tempered and tested by time and experience. In a way, I believed that justice was mine to dispense, rather than relinquishing the injustices I noticed and hated to a merciful and just God who would take care of everything more perfectly than I ever could.

Don't we, as parents, sometimes think that justice is ours to administer to our kids or even on behalf of our kids? If our child is hurting because of a friend's betrayal, we want to swoop in and fix the pain. If our child was wrongfully accused of stealing, we are quick to defend. And, of course in the case of discipline, we equate justice with punishment when our children have offended us or someone else.

Discipline, if done well, involves both justice and mercy. It is not harsh, as we might imagine in our court systems labeled as the judicial branches of our government. Yet it is not permissive, either, but instead leans on the side of compassion. True justice, for us as parents, necessitates an initial surrender through prayer to God about the circumstance of injustice, then discerning through wisdom and grace how we are called to respond.

We can also be examples of the Works of Mercy for our children that, in some small way, right a wrong in our culture. For example, if we discuss the plight of the impoverished with our kids, we might decide as a family to volunteer at our local homeless shelter or food pantry on a regular basis. If littering is a problem in our neighborhood, we might spearhead a monthly clean-up day. If our elected leaders aren't implementing legislature that is moral or ethical, we might schedule an appointment with our local congressman or congresswoman.

There are countless ways we can satiate the hunger and slake the thirst for righteousness, which is a small, but significant, impact on our role as the Body of Christ. Each time we grow in the virtue of justice, we slake Jesus's thirst. He calls us, beckons us with, "I thirst," and we respond in a variety of ways that pertain to our unique family dynamics and individual talents or spiritual charisms.

Instead of doing nothing as we watch our broken and hurting world collapse under the cloud of doubt and despair, we can—and should—do our part to contribute to the healing of society in whatever way God calls us. If we do so as a family, our children will learn important and powerful lessons about what really matters most in life, which is to accompany those who suffer in this world through charity.

How Our Lady Reflected God's Perfect Justice

It's interesting that the Blessed Mother brought about Jesus's public ministry *before his appointed time*. Recall the first miracle to which we attribute the onset of Jesus's ministry: the wedding at Cana. Jesus told Mary, "Woman, my hour has not yet come," but she, in her gentle but persuasive manner, said to the worker, "Do whatever he tells you." Thus, her intercessory work on our behalf began.

Father Jacques Philippe believes the hunger and thirst for righteousness is directly related to how well we persevere in prayer. If we, like the Blessed Mother, tenderly and persistently request that God will accomplish his work before his appointed time, then we are working for God's justice as she did. In fact, he writes, "The Virgin Mary at Cana has the power to speed up the hour of grace."[7]

This is how the Blessed Mother reflected God's perfect justice: she didn't overstep her bounds and never usurped her Son's authority, yet knew she could successfully persuade him to help the couple avoid humiliation on their wedding day. She saw an immediate need, and she asked God to "speed up the hour of grace."

We can do the same if we are imitators of Our Lady. We can see a desperate situation that requires urgent attention and ask God to work more quickly than he might otherwise do. Appealing to his mercy always appeals to his justice, and the Blessed Mother knew this well. Therefore, it's wise for us as mothers to frequently turn to her in desperate times, asking her to plead on our behalf as she did with the newlyweds at Cana, that she might "speed up the hour of grace."

Ben

Hunger and thirst. Those two words can carry a lot of weight, especially as they pertain to our needs and desires. We all thirst for something to drink, as well as hunger for something to eat, but it appears that our society has gone off the rails as to the real meaning of both of these words. We often hear a salesman who's "hungry" for a deal to be made or the stressed-out worker "thirsting" for a vacation. If we put these words in the proper category, then in both of these instances they fall under *desire* and not necessarily a

---

7   Ibid., 129–30.

real *need*. There is certainly a very temporary satisfaction if we look at the worldly view of hunger and thirst.

We need to distinguish between *need* and *desire*. Both of these concepts have been horribly blurred, and all of us, to a degree, have fallen into this misunderstanding. Righteousness is the quality of being morally justified or right. Only God is truly righteous, and since our deepest desire is to be in God's grace, then we all have that same thirst and hunger to be righteous as God is.

Now, it's important to differentiate between what is needed and what is desired. It's easy for us to desire our own definition of righteousness, but it's far more difficult to desire God's righteousness. We can "thirst" for the driver who speeds past us to get caught by the police and have some smug sense of satisfaction, but in the truth of the matter, we may not know that some poor mom is hurrying her child to the emergency room for stitches.

For our own children, we need to distinguish between our sense of righteousness and the real truth of *God's* righteousness. We should show our children that God's will is what truly satisfies us, compared to the temporary satisfaction of our own "hunger." This is a difficult task and requires us to keep our own hunger in check when it comes to our desires and discerning what is truly a thirst for God's righteousness.

We not only need to model a true hunger for righteousness, but we also need to keep an eye on when our children give us cues as to when they are truly hungry. It's easy to see the difference between "May I have a new toy?" as compared to "What happens when I die?" They both show a hunger or thirst for something, but only the latter shows a thirst for

God's righteousness. Not all questions are created with an easy way to make a distinction here, but there should be a thought in the back of our minds as parents to answer the call for that hunger.

For instance, my nephew recently was very distraught about not knowing what happens when he dies. This desire to know is a very real thirst and most certainly a perfect time to address this need to know. As a parent, you don't need an answer to all of life's existential questions right on the tip of your tongue, but don't shy away from answering the difficult questions as they arise. If you don't know the answer right away, don't be afraid to tell your child you'll get them an answer. It shows them that you're willing to be vulnerable but at the same time make the effort to slake their thirst.

To wrap this up in a practical way, by encouraging your children to thirst for the deep questions, you encourage that they build a pattern of *seeking God's righteousness.* The more that they thirst, the more they'll be deeply satisfied. Since you'll not only be feeding them as a parent with answers, you'll teach them about feeding on Jesus in the Eucharist at Mass. Catechize yourself as much as possible, and you'll be able to relay those concepts to your children. The more satisfied they feel with God's righteousness, the less room they'll have for the world to influence their lives.

How St. Joseph Surrendered to God's Justice

How often do we, as parents, pine for God's justice for others but quickly assume mercy for ourselves? We thirst for justice to be done to the person who cut us off in traffic or the lazy coworker, but when we slack at work or in our rush to be somewhere and are less-than-courteous to other drivers, we are quick to excuse our own behavior. Maybe if we reframe our thirst for justice, we can appreciate the difficulties that others face every day.

Once when I was a reserve officer for a local sheriff's department, I was out to deliver justice in the form of a speeding ticket. A woman had pulled past me at a high speed without regard for my marked patrol car, and I was set to make sure that she received the ticket she deserved. As I walked up to the car, I sensed her nervousness. It was a different kind of nervousness than I was used to with my typical traffic stops, so I asked her why she was in such a hurry. She explained that her son had a severe laceration to his head, and she quickly rolled down the tinted window in the rear seat to show me her son, who was holding a bloody towel to his head.

All thoughts of a ticket disappeared as mercy took over in that moment, and I offered any assistance to get her to the hospital quickly (which was very close by). I sent her on her way without a thought of trying to get my slice of justice. If we realize that our expectation of justice and how it will be meted out will always be flawed, then we can trust God in his justice. God has *perfect* justice. Think about that. He allowed his *only* Son to be crucified and tortured, and it was our sins, our imperfect view of justice, and our own willfulness that put those stripes on his back and nails in his hands and feet. Yet it was a sacrifice made perfect. In Christ's humiliation, he knew that God would be perfect in his justice. So, too, should we trust in God and his perfect justice without seeking our own version of it.

In instances that involve justice, I always think of when St. Joseph and Mary found Jesus in the Temple after frantically searching for him. Without humility and resignation to God's will and justice, I think that St. Joseph would have been quite upset and even punished Jesus in some way for his disobedience. But St. Joseph sensed Jesus was in the right because he was in his Father's house, so St. Joseph resigned himself to God's plan.

No justice was warranted on the account of Jesus, and any thoughts that St. Joseph may have borne in his heart and soul were of a human nature that demanded his justice, yet he trusted in God. How many times have we as parents, spouses, and friends felt that we were due some justice in a relationship, situation, or circumstance, yet did not receive it? We need to lean on God and his perfect justice. It may be that the slight that we felt was meant to perfect our soul through trial, and therein lies the true justice of the situation. Maybe a willful child is meant to test our patience, and justice is served in that way rather than how we correct the child. By all means, the child needs correction, but God's justice is always more meritorious than our own version of it.

Bringing Righteousness Into Habit and Home

Sometimes "Mama Bear" comes out when I'm (Jeannie) with my children and I notice people staring at Sarah. It could be a child or adult, but a protective instinct kicks in at a visceral level, which makes me want to shield Sarah from potential harm. That gut feeling often seems like justice to me, as if I have the right somehow verbally to defend Sarah from people's horrified glares. In many ways, I could rationalize doing this. But God says otherwise.

God's justice often doesn't happen according to our timeline or ways. As mothers, we have an inherent desire to fight for our children because we don't want them exposed to woundedness in any way. Maybe our response is related to understanding what betrayal, rejection, and deep misunderstanding feels like, and we don't want that suffering to befall our kids. In turn, justice on a human level is very much saturated in anger and fear—both of which give rise to injustice. Here's how Father Jacques Philippe describes it: "Pursuing a mercantile logic in human relations introduces a kind of violence into relationships. Demanding too much justice sooner or later leads to injustice. Justice unaccompanied by mercy sooner or later becomes injustice."[8]

In a way, then, we have to mirror God's justice in such a way that we cannot separate the gift of mercy that accompanies true justice. What this means for us as parents is that we have to cool off the initial vexation or strong emotional reactions that may lead us to seek revenge rather than God's justice. His timing is perfect, as we know, and it often leads us to pause for a greater length of time before responding.

Perhaps this period of waiting serves the purpose of tempering our emotions so that we can see things more clearly. In turn, our hearts and minds will be at peace, and we will be

---

8   Ibid., 162.

more apt to respond to the unkindness of others with calm compassion rather than frustration or defensiveness.

In the case of inconsiderate people staring at Sarah, I've adopted a benign conversation starter that also serves as an icebreaker when we are in awkward social situations. It's usually evident that the parents are embarrassed when they notice their children gawking at Sarah, and their natural reaction is to sweep them away quickly. Instead, I use that moment as an opportunity for interacting with them.

In mere seconds, I pause, pray, and smile. Then I approach the family and politely offer, "It's okay if you'd like to ask us questions about Sarah." Then I hand them a business card with Sarah's photo and a couple of sentences about her diagnosis in laymen's terms. Most of the time, it is a visible relief to the children and parents, because they know we will welcome their honest questions with equally transparent answers.

This thirst for righteousness we often interpret to mean a thirst for what's right or for *being* right. The way in which we are willing to extend the benefit of the doubt rather than skepticism to others demonstrates our relationship with God too. It means we are seeking an active life of prayer, which deepens our ability for compassion toward others, even in the midst of distressing situations.

Action Plan

Toddlers and Preschoolers

Small children have a natural knack for justice, at least according to their worldview. It's more of a sense of "that's not fair" or wanting everything to be equally distributed (e.g., they are handed five fruit snacks, and so is everyone else). Use natural consequences to teach about God's justice, because they will present themselves to you as a parent without much effort at this age. And, because kids this age are so perceptive, it's a perfect chance for you to foster a sense of *holy* righteousness in them.

Let's say your parish youth ministry is planning a mission trip to help the elderly or disabled in another community. Talk to your small children about how there are some people in the world who need extra help from others. Sometimes what we think is fair isn't actually true love. That will help your children understand that giving *more* or at least what is needed or required, rather than equally, is the actual measure of hungering for God's kingdom on earth.

Elementary Age

When I (Jeannie) was in grade school, the Gulf War was in full swing. As a child who was becoming more aware of what was going on in the world, including a deep-seated sorrow for the war victims, I wanted to do more than just see and know about social injustice. My mom found this great method of allowing me to participate spiritually in the alleviation of other people's suffering. Specifically, I had a coloring page with clouds in a sky, hovering over the war-torn land of the Middle East. Each time I prayed for someone in the war—a soldier, a civilian, or for peace in general—I colored a cloud. Once I filled up the paper with colored clouds,

I started a new one. It was the perfect visual representation of how powerful prayer can be.

You can adapt this kind of activity for whatever concerns your child. Parents, if you are attuned to it, recognize particular areas of interest and care toward which your children gravitate. If it's serving the poor, use a chart with colorful stickers that represent each time the family volunteers at the food pantry or soup kitchen. If it's caring for the elderly or homebound, the chart can be for each time your child makes a homemade card or prays for a special friend who is immobile or infirm.

Adolescence

Teens, because they are usually longing for a cause to believe in, are the perfect demographic to encourage a sense of holy justice through the various Works of Mercy. No longer concrete thinkers alone, they conceptualize far more in the abstract than they did at younger ages. They are ready to serve their community and world actively in unique and purposeful ways.

If you have seen a pattern in what social causes your children prefer already, open and maintain a dialogue about what it means to be the voice of the voiceless and to defend the defenseless in our modern world. Your teen may long to get more involved in the pro-life movement, perhaps by volunteering at the local women's shelter, training to become a counselor, writing inspirational essays, chairing fundraisers for ultrasound equipment, and so on. The point is not so much what the cause is—as long as it is a noble one—as much as it is how you discuss ways your teen and your family can get more involved to make a difference. Adolescents want to make their imprint on the world. We as parents simply have to nudge them a bit and lead by example.

Saint Profile: St. Vincent de Paul

Known as the Great Apostle of Charity, St. Vincent de Paul dedicated his entire apostolate and life to serving the marginalized of society. His thirst for righteousness was met with an active ministry that directly affected the poor, sick, and war victims. Vincent himself was born to a peasant family, and he spent two years captive by pirates who sold him into slavery, so his heartfelt compassion for the suffering and poor was personal.

Over time, with the help of the Daughters of Charity and St. Louise de Marillac, Vincent met poor families in his community and began his ministry by giving them food and spiritual consolation. Eventually large groups of women assisted him, and they became an officially recognized religious congregation known as the Daughters of Charity of Saint Vincent de Paul.

The Vincentians, too, are a religious order of priests dedicated to serving their local communities with whatever needs are present there. Because St. Vincent was deeply concerned about how the Church could and should help those in most need, he inspired others to pursue similar works of charity alongside him. One such charity that thrives in over a hundred countries today is the St. Vincent de Paul Society, an organization that includes food pantries, clothing banks, furniture stores, and programs for payment assistance both at the parish and city levels.

Because St. Vincent de Paul is widely known as the patron of all works of charity, he may be the clearest example of what it means to live out our calling to seek and serve the kingdom of God and its righteousness. We all must begin somewhere, as Vincent did by reaching out to an already-existing group of women who were familiar with the faces and needs of their local poor. From that, he discerned the call to more formal organizations of religious and lay people. And today his work is legendary.

We are all called to sainthood according to the unique path God wants us to pursue. We begin by acknowledging the spark in our hearts, discovering what moves us to create positive change in our world, then discern over time what God is asking us to do about whatever suffering moves us the most. Everyone's call will be different in the way it is lived out. But we can turn to St. Vincent de Paul as both a role model and intercessor as we determine how we, our children, and our families can reach out to a hurting world and slake the thirst for God's righteousness.

Prayer

Heavenly Father, sometimes I am so passionate about what's wrong in the world that I overlook how I might be part of the solution. I know that my baptismal call as a husband, wife, mother, and father means that I might raise the little souls of my children to also work for holy justice. This justice is not out of anger or spite, but rather out of a sense of small increments rather than becoming overwhelmed at its entirety.

Her grace envelops us. When we call upon her, she cloaks us under her mantle of protection and security. It's much easier for me to be patient with my own daughters when I see myself as the daughter of our Blessed Mother and remember how merciful she is with me.

Ben

How hard is it for us to forgive as parents? Do we feel that our children are disobeying us because of their sassy behavior and poor attitude? It's hard as adults to forgive a child since we are so far removed from our own childhood. We see the world through a lens of tasks and checklists rather than a lens of playfulness, innocence, and carefree timelessness. Maybe in some way, our forgiveness, or lack thereof, is related to how deeply entrenched we have become in our own adult world of efficiency and task-oriented thoughts.

Rather than checking a box after spending time with our children, it only takes a moment to come to the level of our children and truly forgive them, but more importantly, to understand their own struggles. Not always, but on many occasions, our children are acting out for attention and through a deep-seated fear or desire. It takes some conversation with and cajoling them to find the right words that bring forth the problems with which they are struggling. Out of a sense of mercy, we seek out these issues and strike at the heart of the matter. This communication builds a richer and more meaningful relationship with our children too.

If your child happens to be the one bullying others, it's important to evaluate the root cause of such behavior. Not many parents are aware when their own children are exhibiting unkind behavior, but if you seek counsel from your pastor and a trusted psychological professional, you will be able to address the issue and better know how to approach changing the behavior.

Begin introducing ways your children can select Corporal Works of Mercy, which are more tangible and simpler to accomplish than the Spiritual Works of Mercy. Consider adopting one or more as a family, such as visiting the sick or elderly, volunteering at a homeless shelter, collecting coats for the poor, etc.

Adolescence

Teens will most likely be ready for deeper concepts of mercy and how to address social issues pertaining to injustice and poverty. It is at this age that you might want to initiate or continue conversations about how they might feel called to alleviate the suffering of others. This action can be as simple as consoling a classmate who has lost a parent or sending cards or letters to someone in prison through a prison minister or chaplain. If your teenager expresses interest in more global concerns, such as raising money for people in impoverished areas to have access to clean water, you might discuss the possibility of your teen (or entire family) going on a mission trip.

There are a variety of resources to help you and your teen decide what options might be the best fit and how to prepare for such a trip. Catholic Relief Services is one such resource. If you'd prefer to remain within the United States, Catholic Heart Work Camp is a domestic youth mission trip that your child can plug into during summer break once per year.

Teenagers will better understand and be able to participate in the Spiritual Works of Mercy, such as counseling the doubtful, instructing the ignorant, and admonishing the sinner. All of these can, and should, be done in a spirit of charity and respect. Roleplay possible conversations your teen may have with their peers about the Catholic Church or religion in general and how to respond mercifully. Helping your children to react mercifully to these situations is also a great evangelization tool.

Saint Profile: St. Teresa of Calcutta

Most modern Catholics are familiar with St. Teresa's story. She was a beloved public figure in the 1980s and '90s, and now she is a well-loved, newly canonized saint. Teresa was born Agnes to an Albanian family and became a Loreto nun at the age of eighteen. When she completed her novitiate in Darjeeling, India, she initially taught at the privileged girls' school the sisters led on the premises of their convent.

Teresa had been drawn to missionary life as a young girl, and her missionary spirit never stopped burning in her heart. At times, she would glance outside the convent school window and sorrowfully watch the villagers in their everyday lives. She noticed their poverty, and it pierced her heart so deeply that she impulsively brought a group of them food from the convent one evening.

After Teresa was chastised by her Mother Superior, she explained that she felt something must be done to assuage the plight of the poor who surrounded the sisters' community. Shortly thereafter, Teresa caught a train to make a retreat. While on the train, she distinctly and clearly heard God tell her to alleviate the needs of the poorest of the poor. She called this her "call within a call" and brought the message back home to her Mother Superior.

St. Teresa knew she was to found an order with an apostolate that directly served the needs of the forgotten, unloved, and dying. But founding that order was no ordinary task and proved to be quite a feat. Even so, she persevered by living within the bounds of her religious vows and never veered away from the orders she received from her superiors.

For a time, she was granted temporary permission to mingle and live among the poorest of the poor. At first, she worked alone, establishing relationships and building trust among the villagers she served. She often fed those who were hungry by giving up her own meals. She educated the children who longed to understand how to read and write. And she attended to those who were sick, dying, or in otherwise desperate situations.

She is a saint of mercy because she recognized the poverty of loneliness above all else. St. Teresa didn't want anyone to die alone and forgotten. As she gained permission to found her order, other young women joined her efforts as schools and the Home for the Dying were established. Among the religious factions in India, common folk trusted her because she never tried to convert anyone to Christianity.

St. Teresa loved everyone wholeheartedly. That is what transformed the hearts of the poor and those who worked with her or interacted with her. It was the fact that she intentionally worked with and tenderly cared for those who were filthy, reeking of death and disease. She didn't walk away in horror, no matter how difficult it was to face the condition of the persons she encountered.

She met them at the heart of who they were. She saw the dignity of each person, regardless of race, socioeconomic status, or creed, and she loved them all with equal care and concern. St. Teresa can be considered a stellar role model of mercy, a true exemplar of what it means to deliberately go into our communities, seek those who are lost and forsaken, and love them.

Prayer

Heavenly Father, there are so many saints who taught us what your mercy looks like in action and daily life. Through the intercession of St. Teresa of Calcutta, we ask that you open our hearts to the suffering souls surrounding us every day. These might be people we often overlook or otherwise wouldn't want to stop and help. But help us to see your face in them so that we might alleviate their pain in some small way. Grant us clarity and purpose in our mission as a family, and help us to grow in kindness and mercy as we forgive each other and learn from each other. Amen.

CHAPTER 6

Blessed Are the Pure of Heart, for They Will See God

A pure heart is turned toward God, not the self.

—Father Jacques Philippe[11]

Jeannie

One whose heart is pure is one who is childlike and innocent and whose spirituality is uncomplicated and unstained by the weight of life's baggage. Don't we all tend to carry some sort of emotional burden into adulthood? Purity of heart, however, is a return to innocence by way of simplicity of faith. It also involves selflessness, a total giving of oneself through altruism.

I can honestly say that I became purer of heart the instant I became a mom. When I was pregnant with Felicity, I began to understand what it meant to give of myself completely,

---

11   Jacques Philippe, *The Eight Doors to the Kingdom*, 170.

without restraint or conditions. I gave my entire body to nourish and protect her, despite the discomforts of pregnancy. Once she was born, I had given my body again to deliver her through labor pains and the opening of my womb so that she could safely enter the world. And, as I healed from the delivery, I gave all of myself to her—my sleep, my eating priorities, and my time—so that she could be fed, cuddled, and clean.

Some people say there's no such thing as pure altruism, but spiritually speaking, it can be attained. My heart has been refined time and again as a mom because my girls inadvertently stretch me to become less lazy and more generous. Becoming one who is pure of heart isn't easy, however. It takes quite a bit of refining in the crucible of suffering and self-denial! As parents, we are called to give of ourselves, even to die to our former way of living. And this giving is no small task. But, through God's goodness and grace, we can achieve that state of childlike innocence again through the act of selfless giving.

When Felicity was a newborn, I fell prey to discouragement, realizing that I was a selfish person who sought comfort through sleep, eating at specific times, and doing what I wanted on my own time. I didn't see how egocentric I truly was until I was thrust into this new rhythm of nursing her every two hours, thinking of what was best for her and thus relinquishing some of my ministerial activities that happened in the evenings, and holding her when I would have preferred to curl up alone with a good book.

Purity of heart is something that is natural for our children. They are born innocent and only become jaded by life as they enter the age of reason and learn that betrayals happen, people disappoint, and life isn't fair. When they are young, however, the world is full of wonder and all is fresh and new. Life is beautiful because it isn't filled with complex responsibilities. And that wonder, that innocence, leads us to yearn for purity of heart too.

I recall one specific point in time when I was wrestling with the trenches of new motherhood. It was a Sunday, and Ben and I took Felicity to Mass, but she was fussing loudly. Before we arrived at church, I had hoped to be able to participate in Mass somewhere other than the cry room for the first time in several months, but my hopes were dashed as I exited the pew and rocked her back and forth on the way to the back of church.

Felicity was about eighteen months old at the time, approaching those oft-dreaded years of terrible twos and threes. She wanted to be held rather than walk, so I carried her past the statues and icons adorning the walls and alcoves of our parish. Suddenly, her fussing ceased, and her face lit up. Her eyes sparkled and grin widened as an image of Our Lady caught her attention. She was enraptured.

"Mama Mary," she said, pointing and smiling. I nodded and watched her closely. "Mama Mary loves me," she continued softly. I nodded again, mesmerized by this simple but profound interaction. Then she proceeded to talk gibberish to the image of Our Lady of Guadalupe, using words and phonetic syllables that only the divine could interpret.

In that moment, I knew Felicity was truly speaking to "Mama Mary" with her heart. I just knew it. I could see it in that love she carried for her spiritual mother. And suddenly, though I missed the entire Liturgy of the Word, including the homily, I realized I had gained a homily of my own in the sacrament of the present moment. There, with my "demanding" toddler (so I thought at the time), I was schooled in what it meant to love with a heart that is pure, open, and receptive to all that God has in store for it.

From that moment onward, Felicity was enthralled with every image or statue she saw of Our Lady. We did teach her about "Mama Mary," but we didn't purposefully expose her to every single version of her that existed. Still, Felicity intuited the comforting presence of her spiritual mother, and I, in turn, was consoled in my difficulties as a new mother. Slowly, steadily, my heart began to change—not necessarily all at once, and not without lots of trial and error—but I became transformed from the inside out.

I learned that purity of heart meant that I must always be willing and ready to receive the Lord, no matter the circumstances. I had to be able to see with the eyes of an open heart, to have a heart that was clean and capable of recognizing God in the overlooked ordinary happenings of everyday life as a mom. Yes, in the midst of cleaning and cooking and changing diapers and calming inconsolable cries, I had to discover God's presence as my little sweet daughter had done so readily.

If we are receptive to it, our hearts will change when we become parents. This change begins from the moment of our child's conception, yes, but it can continue to flourish well beyond our early parenting days if we allow it to. By grace of the sacrament of our parenthood, God leads us out of our complicated cynicism and worry, beyond the daily grind and onerous responsibilities and into a world of enchantment and wonder again—into the eternal. That is purity of heart. It is a journey we take together with our children, a lifelong journey toward heaven.

The Immaculate Conception: Role Model for Purity

Because Mary was conceived without the stain of original sin, she dispenses particular graces related to purity under the title Immaculate Conception. She herself was guileless in all ways and perfect in virtue from the moment she was conceived in her mother's womb (called "prevenient grace"),[12] which makes the Immaculate Conception an ideal devotion for those of us who have kids entering adolescence.

Truthfully, we can begin invoking her intercession when our children are very young. It's no secret that children are exposed to countless forms of impurities when they are very young. As a result, we become overwhelmed at the prospect of shielding them from such atrocities, and yet we do have access to the one woman, above all other saints in heaven, who is waiting for us to seek her help for our children.

To cultivate devotion the Immaculate Conception, try watching the *Song of Bernadette* as a family. To follow up, read about the life of St. Bernadette Soubirous and explain how the Blessed Mother revealed herself as the Immaculate Conception to Bernadette. Research different miracles that have taken place at Lourdes, and relate to your children how

---

12   Fr. Cyprian, "Immaculate Conception and Pervenient Grace," New Camaldoli Hermitage, accessed May 3, 2018, https://contemplation.com/immaculate-conception-and-prevenient-grace/.

important it is for our souls to be clean in order for us to reach heaven.

Pray to the Immaculate Conception daily for your children's purity to be preserved. There are many prayers specific to Mary under this title that can be found in Catholic bookstores and online. One example is to schedule your Marian Consecration for the Feast of the Immaculate Conception, December 8. You can also pray a novena preceding the feast day.

Remember that God has given you spiritual authority over your children according to natural and divine law. Because of this authority, you can pray the Marian Consecration on behalf of your children if they are particularly detached from the idea. The effects of grace will still be given to them as if they prayed with full devotion as an act of the will. Naturally, you will want to continue to encourage personal prayer to the Blessed Mother, which opens the heart to vast graces.

Ben

Men are visual creatures. Draw us a diagram, show us a blue print, a picture or some other physical representation of what you're trying to convey, and we'll get it. Since we are visual, we also have a weakness that comes with this strength. The very same visual connection that allows our imagination to be creative can also be quite the cross to bear if we're not careful. It becomes very important for us as men and fathers to guard our eyes and thoughts when it comes to the opposite sex.

Modesty is a word that we rarely hear anymore but certainly applies to men and women alike. As men and fathers, we must be sure to guide our children properly in modest dress and also show our children that we are aware of immodesty around us and how to avoid it, if possible. My oldest daughter, Felicity, picked up on modesty quite quickly and was very fast to point out women who were immodestly dressed at the grocery store. She did so quite loudly on several occasions, much to Jeannie's embarrassment. The point is that she was able to pick up on what is and is not appropriate and quickly make the connection.

On the road to modesty, we have a goal in mind. That goal is *purity*. Purity of thought, purity of intention, and purity of action are how I like to further break down purity into specific areas.

Let's start with purity of thought, in which we maintain custody of the *mind*. Spend a day intentionally trying to maintain purity of thought. Hard, isn't it? You'll quickly realize that what you feed into your mind has a much greater effect on your thoughts than you realize.

Advertisers know this, and that's why you're fed a steady diet of images, words, and videos to sway your thoughts and emotions. By coming to this realization, you should spend some time in prayer and meditation on all the ways that you're easily manipulated by the various streams of media and work on minimizing contact with them. When we made this realization, both Jeannie and I made the conscious decision to get rid of cable TV altogether. It may sound difficult, but I honestly do not miss television at all. If I'm going to watch something, it is specific and not mindless flipping of channels. By doing this, I am more aware of my thoughts and don't allow them to be so easily influenced by people or circumstances.

Purity of intention is another area that should be in forefront of your mind as a parent. Think for a moment of all the intentional choices that you make each day. Do those choices have an intent that is *pure,* or are there deep-seated, sinful reasons as to why you do something? Do you allow your children to watch another movie so you don't have to hear them whine about how they want to watch more TV? Trust me, I'm not saying that anyone is a bad parent because of a choice like that; I'm just trying to illustrate the point that purity of intention is hard to master.

Maybe you talk to a coworker who likes to gossip. It helps you get away from some paperwork you'd rather avoid and gives you the "scoop" on current rumors. Begin to question your own motives, and you'll begin to see patterns emerge in the choices that you make. Recognizing these patterns will help you to make choices that have an actual purity of *intention.* You will then model to your children the hard choices you have to make since there can be a sting to your pride or a heavy dash of humility (like changing that horrible diaper disaster so that your wife doesn't have to deal with the "nuclear waste" situation).

Lastly, we look at purity of *action.* Purity of action is where purity of thought and purity of intent converge. It's really a progression to where you work on thinking pure thoughts, intending to do something without duplicity, and then putting them both into action. One such example is that I had some extra spending money in my wallet that I was going to use to buy beer on the way home. I ended up hanging onto it and donating it to church during Adoration as the small offering to light some votive candles for my family. I thought that the money may be better used by the Church and that prayers for my family would be better spent than on myself. I intended to do this without regret or thought of myself, and finally I let go of the money without a second thought.

It's a fairly ordinary example, but starting with something small can lead to bigger and bigger sacrifices made by you as a father. Once again, children notice these things, even if they don't grasp the true significance right away. On your journey through this life, you'll begin to see God in more and more areas of your life by putting into practice these small steps. This ability to see God at work in your life is the *fruit* of purity of heart. I know I have a very long way to go in achieving purity, but it's achievable, and no matter how many times I fall, I pick myself up and begin again.

The Purity of St. Joseph

This world loves to mock the sixth and ninth commandments. At every turn, you're faced with billboards, internet ads, and TV and radio commercials that sexualize everything from hamburgers to shaving products. It's a constant stream of temptation that not only makes it hard to pursue the virtuous life for parents but also creates a toxic environment for children who have less life experience to deal with the mixed emotions brought on by the bilge pumps of society.

As parents, it becomes quite clear that we need to show our children how to keep custody of their minds, as well as their senses, and especially their sight. The eyes are the "window to the soul," which makes it much more imperative to make sure our children know what to gaze upon and what to look away from. Taking a cue from St. Joseph, who is the Terror of Demons, we should be that terror as fathers too. Don't be afraid to terrorize unchaste thoughts in your own daily life with prayers of purity.

By working on your own purity and modeling that to your children, they will take your lead and begin to emulate your own chastity and pursuit of purity. Do you have pornography in the house or anything that objectifies women? Terrorize it, and remove it immediately. Not only is it the near occasion of sin, but it gives your children, especially your daughters, the wrong idea of what they need to do to attract the male sex. In a state of mortal sin? Terrorize the demons of lust and impurity with confession and a firm purpose of amendment never to fall into the temptation of objectifying women.

To illustrate the point in which impurity and lust can be such a huge burden, I was given a perfect example by a priest. He spoke of a story where two monks were traveling between monasteries and came to a river that they needed to cross. As they approached the river, there was a woman standing there alone and looking for help to get to the other side. The woman was quite beautiful, and one of the monks stared at her for quite some time, engraving her beauty in his mind. The elder of the monks offered to carry her across the river and did so with a joyful heart.

Once on the other side of the river, the woman thanked the monks and went on with her journey. As the two monks continued walking, the younger of the monks thought more and more of this woman and how beautiful she was. After some time, the younger monk verbalized how beautiful the woman was, but the elder monk replied, "My brother, I only carried the woman across the river, but you have shouldered her as a burden for much longer than I on this journey."

As fathers, we must loosen the burden of impurity on our hearts and souls. Only then can we be unhindered in carrying our children across childhood and into adulthood.

Bringing Purity of Heart Into Habit and Home

When we think of purity, we automatically associate bodily chastity and modesty with this beatitude. While these are certainly part of a heart that is innocent and does not want to offend God, they don't comprise the entirety of living the beatitude. We believe the exterior expressions of modest dress and chaste behavior must begin in the heart.

Purity of heart is directly related to uprightness, simplicity, and unity with God.[13] When one's heart is pure, it is not distracted by frivolities or extraneous distractions. In our modern milieu, we tend to make everything too complicated: our food choices at the grocery store, "necessities" for new babies, digital clutter on our devices, and even the danger of living by our fickle and complex emotions.

This beatitude beckons us to return to the virtues related to what is unblemished by overthinking, overanalyzing, and

---

[13]   Jacques Philippe, *The Eight Doors to the Kingdom*, 169.

exaggeration. Think back on the first beatitude, poverty of spirit. Purity of heart points back to the very foundation of our walk through the Beatitudes as parents because it is an invitation to rid ourselves of the excess that weighs us down spiritually, emotionally, and physically.

Purity of heart is a tough beatitude to practice in Western culture because we are so immersed in the consumeristic mindset. For many of us, the acquisition of material possessions, a cushy career with plenty of vacation days and comfortable salary, or living in a fancy home has become the norm. We seldom question these things, especially within our own families.

But if you're reading this book, it's likely that you want to do some spiritual renovations in your family. This beatitude will help you because it is a gradual type of surrender or detachment from all that draws us away from God.

Father Jacques Philippe explains that "purity of heart illuminates life and transforms one's way of thinking"[14] and it is "above all a matter of orientation. . . . Nothing purifies the heart so much as praising and blessing God."[15] When we make a habit of thanking God for the abundant blessings in our life, we are approaching the essence of this beatitude.

In our family, we've tried a simple formula that kickstarts our older girls into thinking about prayer as conversation with God. Instead of a mechanical lesson, we offer them prompts that make them think about their day and address the four hallmarks of prayer (adoration/praise, contrition,

---

[14]   Ibid., 167.
[15]   Ibid., 173.

thanksgiving, and supplication/petition). It's akin to a mini examination of conscience.

First, we have them say, "Dear Jesus, my day was . . . " which helps them reflect on the general sense of how their day went. We are always surprised when the girls offer a very specific insight that signals they really do understand that they struggled that day or had a really spectacular time. Next, they pray, "Thank you for . . . " which obviously focuses on the importance of gratitude. After that, it's "I'm sorry for . . ." because we feel that children need to address what went wrong or could have been done better. Finally, they pray, "Please help me to . . . " which concludes the prayer with petition.

This prayer is deliberate and sounds quite natural when prayed. Our oldest has chosen to pray silently rather than aloud, but Sarah still needs a lot of prompting to jog her memory. Both options are okay. The point is to get your children to ponder their lives in a supernatural sense, in light of eternity. We begin with praise and gratitude because it fosters this purity of heart.

Action Plan

Toddlers and Preschoolers

Children at this age are naturally open to spiritual matters. They are most likely to be attentive to the unseen world and might surprise you with questions or comments about angels and saints. Don't dissuade or discourage these comments, even if you find them to be incredible or outlandish. Listen openly and add brief comments about God and the afterlife as needed. You will probably discover that you learn much from your child's purity of heart—openness to God's workings in the world—that will then open your own heart too.

Elementary Age

It's getting more difficult to protect and preserve your child's innocence as he or she gets older. Inevitably, the influence of culture and the school environment will at least minimally creep into his or her psyche and behavior. Without completely sheltering your son or daughter in a proverbial bubble, it is possible to retain that purity of heart, at least to some degree. For one, continue to provide a solid faith foundation in your home. Faithfully attend Mass on Sundays and Holy Days.

If you aren't already, find ways you can get involved in your parish community through various ministries. Encourage your child to develop a personal prayer life. (You can do this by teaching various forms of prayer as described in the previous section—adoration/praise, contrition, thanksgiving, and supplication/petition. You can also explain that prayer is really conversation with God as a friend.)

Pray together as a family. Talk about current world events and issues that affect your children. Monitor what shows, movies, music, and video games they are exposed to and discuss with them why you are opposed to certain forms of entertainment (e.g., based on nudity, unnecessary violence, bad language, etc.). There are myriad other ways you can facilitate holiness in your child; pray about what might work best for you and your situation.

Adolescence

By this point, your son or daughter has definitely learned about scandals and corruption due to tidbits of conversations and even possibly exposure at teen parties. Open the conversation by asking your child what's going on with other kids their age. You can do this casually by saying, "I noticed a lot of young people think drinking at parties is a fun way to hang out and maybe even makes them look more daring to others. What do you think about that?" There are various forms of this question for a variety of topics, such as premarital sex, drug use, pornography, lying, cheating, stealing, etc. It's never too late to begin this conversation, however awkward it may feel. It will especially be tough if you are just now starting to foster virtue in your children.

Purity of heart, akin to innocence, is also about openness. Some teens might think it's lame to pray or be open to the promptings of the Holy Spirit, but if they aren't far removed from their confirmation, it's a good idea to reintroduce the gifts and fruits of the Holy Spirit and how God might be calling them to deepen their faith. It's also a great opportunity to discuss different vocations and encourage your teen to be open to the priesthood, religious or consecrated life, or marriage.

Saint Profile: St. Thérèse of Lisieux

Who better to showcase the beatitude of purity in spirit than the well-beloved Little Flower? Her simplicity radiated the innocence of heart she carried for Jesus, and because of this innocence, her spirituality and timeless wisdom have transformed people's lives for over a century and a half.

Therese had a rough beginning to her life, as her primary caregiver was a nurse instead of her mother, Zélie. Therese had frail health, and Zélie was unable to care adequately for Therese the first two years of her life. Perhaps being cared for by a nurse rather than her mother was why Thérèse became such a sensitive little girl, crying easily and becoming quickly hurt over small grievances.

Sadly, Zélie passed away when Thérèse was only four years old. The fragility of life became a source of grief for little Therese, who was stricken with sadness and longing for security. Her oldest sister, Pauline, became her surrogate mother and educated little Thérèse at home. Until she was nine years old, Therese was often flung into deep melancholic moods that resulted in tantrums and crying fits.

At the age of nine, however, her life drastically transformed. Pauline entered the Carmelite convent, which little Thérèse interpreted to mean that she was being abandoned yet again. That same year, Thérèse fell gravely ill and was bedridden for months with a mysterious illness that was never medically diagnosed.

On the precipice of death, Thérèse turned her face toward a statue of Our Lady that was near her bedside and prayed in desperation to be cured. In that instant, Mary's face radiated with love and mercy, and Thérèse soon thereafter made a full recovery. She referred to this statue as "Our Lady of the Smile."

After this healing, Thérèse also experienced spiritual healing. Her crying fits and mood swings ceased. She became aware of a clear calling to join the Carmelites as a cloistered nun, though she was only nine years old. Shortly after declaring this to her family, she added, "I was born for glory," a bold and zealous statement for a young child who was destined for incredible sanctity.

Therese's life as a young lady in her teen years proved to be trying, both spiritually and physically. She was granted permission to enter Carmel at the age of fifteen, which was unheard of even then. Her dark night of the soul consisted of a deep chasm of loneliness and sense of being abandoned by God. Still, she never revealed these feelings to anyone, except by obedience to her superiors in a notebook that became her spiritual memoir, *The Story of a Soul.*

Physical maladies afflicted Thérèse too. She hid them well and offered everything as a gift to God. She is famously attributed as saying, "Everything is grace," and this indeed was her life's motto. Regardless of the misfortune, rejection she received from other nuns in her cloister, or illnesses that left her stricken with pain, Therese offered everything as a gift of love for the One who first loved her.

And this love became the foundation of her beautiful and pure interior life. Her heart was so radiant and untainted that she was able to formulate an incredible theology around her "little way" of giving small, daily deeds to God each day through hidden acts of love. It's likely that is why she is one of the most popular and beloved saints of all time, because she didn't preach a complex gospel or advocate for great intellectual heights. Instead, she touched the hearts of common people with her childlike faith and confidence in God.

We, as parents, can turn to Thérèse in two main ways. One, we can ask for her intercession upon our children's faith journey. Because Thérèse struggled with emotional immaturity and was easily frustrated as a child, for our strong-willed children, she can be a beacon and mentor to assist them in spiritual maturity. Two, we can pray that St. Thérèse will guide our hearts as moms and dads so that we may become childlike in our worldview once again in order to reach the hearts of our children and recognize and foster their innate sense of encountering God through simple means.

Prayer

Holy Spirit, open my eyes that I might see my children as you see them. Open my ears that I might engage in holy conversation with them about what matters most and least in life. Open my mind that I might notice what bothers them and how to allay their fears and worries. Open my hands that I might serve them with selfless generosity. Open my lips that I might speak words of wisdom and truth to them. And above all, open my heart to know your voice and respond to the ways you are calling me to guide my children to heaven so that they one day might be with you eternally. Amen.

CHAPTER 7

Blessed Are the Peacemakers, for They Will Be Called Children of God

Placing this Beatitude seventh signifies that one who lives according to the six that precede it will receive the grace of peace.

—Father Jacques Philippe[16]

Jeannie

P eace is something most parents long for, especially during the tumultuous times of raising children (and let's be honest: what stages *aren't* tumultuous). Recently, I was packing boxes of baby items, clothing, and a hodge-podge of ephemera in our home of nearly ten years. I did this with a bulging pregnant belly and two young children who seek incessant attention. On a pretty much daily basis, I get bombarded with a plethora of questions (some interesting,

---

[16]   Jacques Philippe, *The Eight Doors to the Kingdom*, 182.

some mundane or even repetitive), lots of requests to read books (the same ones over and over again), and I get interrupted constantly with scuffles between the girls that I need to mediate.

Peace is a gift—and spiritual fruit—I often pray for, though it seems mostly intangible these days. As I packed our belongings for the move, I wondered, as we approached the time of welcoming our third daughter into the world, if peace would be even more of a distant mockery, or if we really could attain it as a family.

I've come to understand that peace is something for which we must first pray. It's a lot like forgiveness: even when we are still feeling angry or unsettled, we can ask God for the grace to *want* to forgive or to desire peace. If you're a natural introvert like I am, you are probably already at the point of begging God out of desperation for a moment's peace. From day to day, I long for the girls' bedtime simply so that I can regain control of my brain again!

Every parent is called to be a peacemaker. We moderate fights; we encourage sharing; we dole out equal measures of snacks. Even beyond these, parents discover that peacemaking involves fostering interior peace in our home life and marriage, which means security, stability, and harmony in our hearts and homes.

When I was a young adult in college, I often heard the word "peace" used synonymously with "unity." As I grew older, however, I realized that peace cannot merely be the absence of discord. At times, working as a peacemaker includes asking tough questions, speaking hard truths, and ruffling feathers. Cultivating peace does not mean we avoid conflict and remain huddled in our comfort zones. Instead, we have to stretch a bit—maybe a lot, depending on temperament—and find a way to teach our children that working for peace requires grit, grace, and a lot of courage.

Felicity is our little peacemaker. She is an inherently sensitive child, constantly aware of other people's sufferings and tension that may be festering in any human dynamic. As a result, she often brings to the fore of a conversation the very issues that adults surrounding her are trying to avoid bringing up for discussion. Sometimes she asks those blunt questions to get the ball rolling, but other times she will point out what she observes happening: someone is sad or frustrated, another person is stressed or overwhelmed, and so on.

She is like a spiritual and emotional barometer in our home, indicating the health of our family. What's beautiful about her giftedness in this area is that she, at the age of seven, already realizes that working toward harmony often entails honest, difficult discussions. We have to work through our issues and come to a respectful and mutual conclusion before we can truly be at peace with one another.

Therefore, working for peace as parents often means we must educate ourselves and our children about the issues that don't always make sense to us. Sometimes these will be social concerns, but other times we simply have to ask each other to clarify what they mean so that we can come to a greater compassion for the people we interact with on a daily basis.

To be at peace within one's own heart and soul is another matter too. But it seems that when we are striving for peace in our families and communities, we must also seek it in ourselves. A restless heart cannot authentically live as a peacemaker. Duplicity is very transparent, especially to our children.

Living the spirituality of peace often means we must learn self-sacrifice and practice it daily, live in total trust of God's providence in taking care of the details of our lives, and abandon our need for control into God's hands. When we relinquish to God the process, timing, and outcome of every situation we face, we necessarily are settled in soul.

For those of us who are type A control freaks (like I am), peace does not come easily. One Scripture verse that has been particularly consoling to me when I find myself feeling anxious, fretting over pettiness, and snapping at everyone around me is from Philippians 4:6–7: "Have no anxiety at all, but in everything, by prayer and petition, with thanks-giving, make your requests known to God. Then the peace of God that surpasses all understanding will guard your hearts and minds in Christ Jesus."

When Sarah had her first surgery at the age of six months, I was worried that I wouldn't worry about it. It's irrational, I know, but I was of the mindset that I *should* worry and have my interior peace be disturbed. As a baby, I didn't want her to undergo such a risky surgery that involved reconstructing her skull. But I knew that without the surgery, she was at risk for brain damage and even possible death.

As the surgical team wheeled Sarah into the operating room and Ben and I kissed her little forehead goodbye, we slowly sauntered into the surgical waiting area, a place rife with anxious waiting and heavy sighs. I settled in with my prayer books and laptop, Ben with his work. As I thought about what was happening to Sarah—something entirely beyond our control—I realized that my heart was completely at rest. I was not worrying. I was at peace, the grace of a supernatural peace that left a newfound confidence lingering in my hear that God was caring for Sarah through the competent surgical team.

In essence, peace must begin within our own hearts. And we can attain it through fervent, consistent prayer. Peace often comes to us when we experience and demonstrate forgiveness too. And when we are at peace within ourselves, we can then continue to be those peacemaker parents who settle arguments between our kids, explain to them how to come to a truce or mutual understanding, and even strive for bigger social justice issues that affect our community and culture.

Don't be concerned if your life feels chaotic and messy. Mine sure does. I'm not sure that will change on the outside, but what I do know is that I keep coming back to my inner sanctuary when I pray in solitude each morning. And that is where God fills me with his peaceful presence, renewed and energized for the day's work as mommy-peacemaker. The point is that we continue to seek and pursue peace, even when life is uncertain and arduous.

Our Lady, Queen of Peace

In sixteenth-century France, a young couple received as a wedding gift a beautiful statue of the Blessed Mother holding an olive branch in one hand and cradling the Prince of Peace in the other arm. It became a beloved family heirloom, known as the "Virgin of Joyeuse" after the family surname. The couple's grandson, Jean Joyeuse, joined the Capuchins in 1588 and took the statue with him to the Capuchin community in Paris, where it remained for two hundred years. It was during this time the beautiful Virgin was affectionately titled and venerated "Notre Dame de Paix," or "Our Lady of Peace."

As time progressed, people from all walks of life, including King Louis XIV and Pope Alexander VII, came to pray to Our Lady of Peace for specific requests. During the French Revolution, the Capuchins were forced to flee their community in Paris, but they took the beloved statue with them. Once peace was restored, they gave it to a religious community, the Congregation of the Sacred Hearts of Jesus and Mary and the Perpetual Adoration of the Blessed Sacrament. These priests, brothers, and sisters then erected a chapel to honor Our Lady of Peace and enshrined the Renaissance-style wooden statue there.[17]

Devotion to the Blessed Mother under this title has exponentially grown through the centuries. Today, the title is included in the Litany of Loreto, and specific novenas to invoke the fruit of peace from her Spouse, the Holy Spirit, are popular. Because her feast day is on July 9, devotees begin their novena on June 30. Here is an excerpt from one of the daily prayers:

---

[17]   Louis Yim, "The Saga of Our Lady of Peace," *Hawii Catholic Herald*, July 4, 2014, http://www.hawaiicatholicherald.com/2014/07/04/the-saga-of-our-lady-of-peace/

> Hail, thou most sublime Queen of Peace, most holy
> Mother of God! By the Sacred Heart of Jesus, thy Son,
> the "Prince of Peace," appease His anger and obtain
> that He may reign over us in peace.

In a world enthralled with violence and a media that preys upon stories evoking fear and division in the populace, we would do well to turn to Our Lady, Queen of Peace often. We know that Satan has focused his efforts on separating marriages and bringing strife into families, and perhaps we have experienced some of this heartbreak ourselves. If we turn to our Blessed Mother under this title, we do so with confidence that she will restore healing and peace to our lives and homes.

Ben

When we think of peace, what springs to mind? Is it the absence of war (which is not peace at all, but I digress) or a life that is free from strain and stress? Is it being financially stable with a sense of knowing you'll be free from money troubles? In the end, it's none of these situations. Interior peace is the goal, and it is a far more secure state of life than anything aforementioned.

You cannot become a peacemaker until you've pushed hard through prayer and mortification to find that *interior* peace. It's also a life-changing experience once you have a glimpse of how spiritually filling the peace of *Christ* can be. In searching for that peace of heart, you find many things in your life stripped away: hobbies, friends (who actually never were friends), and attachments of all sorts. You are given a sudden awareness of your character flaws.

For husbands and fathers, the pursuit of this interior peace is paramount to becoming the peacemaker in the family. Children easily pick up on the mood of grumpy parents or sense that something may be wrong. It is incumbent on the father to strive for interior peace so that there can be a sense of stability for the wife and children, while also offering them a model for the pursuit of their own peace.

I recently had one of the most fruitful Lenten seasons in recent memory, and it was not because I kept all my resolutions on what to give up but because I took a serious look at myself. For example, I have used humor as a double-edged sword much of my life both to conceal a partial truth as well as to cut deeply with something funny (but with a hard edge of judgment). Even though it took a long time to come to the surface, it was a deep realization that I have been duplicitous in the sense that I was not fully humorous or fully honest to others in charity.

Knowing this was hard but brought a sense of peace and clarity because I knew I had something to work on. It was also a realization that through humor that cut deeply, I was disturbing the peace of those around me, especially Jeannie. Interior peace is a journey, and as we pursue virtue and root out defects in our life, we take little steps towards the peace of Christ. Lots of prayer to Our Lady of Sorrows, asking her to point out our defects, is one of the most surefire means of obtaining peace through clarity in self-awareness.

Not only does a search for our defects help us become peacemakers, but trust in God does as well. There will be lots of points in your marriage and with your children that require trust with you putting everything in God's hands. Being honest enough with yourself to say that you don't have all the answers and turning to God is a lesson that cannot be shown enough to your wife and children. The humility to model this honesty is one of the fruits of interior peace. Let me assure you it's very hard to do, and humility is not something that comes easily to most people, but it is achievable. Being a peacemaker takes lots of time and realization that the journey to heaven is a long stream of humilities that build the bridge to heaven.

Another act of humility that helps nudge you towards inner peace is the sacrament of Reconciliation. Make an effort to go once a month and build it into a habit. By showing your children that confession is a worthwhile pursuit, you model a path to interior peace. By going to confession regularly, you also gain a great catharsis in being forgiven, which should also point towards forgiving others. It's a cycle that bears much fruit and turns you into a peacemaker.

I remember a recent confession that felt like a serious spiritual house cleaning, and it was a very intense, but the weight lifted from my shoulders was immense. You do not realize the baggage that you can carry with you over time if you do not put your sins into the hands of Christ. As a father, your family will feel the effects of the weight lifted from your shoulders and there will be more peace in your home than you thought possible. The daily grind will not disappear, but the ability for yourself and your family to feel an interior peace, no matter the circumstance, will quickly prove to be invaluable.

St. Joseph the Peacemaker

I always find it amusing that certain trends that are considered countercultural, such as tattoos, suddenly find their way into societal mainstream and are no longer against the norm. In fact, *not* to have a tattoo is countercultural! If you want to be a peacemaker, then you must have some anchor by which you can gauge your position, an immovable anchor that will remain, no matter how quickly society crumbles or shifts around you must be what grounds you in faith.

St. Joseph was in shock to find that Mary was bearing a child, so the hardness of the hearts in society pushed him to consider stoning her to death for adultery. While that may have seemed like an "anchor" in society, the dream of St. Gabriel revealed a greater truth. Gabriel's words were the *true* anchor in which St. Joseph was grounded. That which comes from God is the greatest of anchors, and by leaning on the Holy Spirit for wisdom, knowledge, and prudence, we can become the greatest of peacemakers in our family.

Swimming against the societal tide as a father can be quite difficult. We may become a peacemaker in our own home but quickly become *persona non grata* in social circles or other areas of our life. Our anchor in God and his truth may be mocked, sneered at, or given complete indifference, but in the face of such negativity, fortitude is a necessary aspect of being a peacemaker. We may attempt to make peace with God's truth, but those who reject it will feel no such peace and may even have a sense of anger that they're all too willing to express towards you.

Be a peacemaker in your own heart when you become the object of societal anger. Understand that this road is hard, but Jesus has already walked it, leaving a trail of blood for you to follow. Stay the course and do not let the gale-force winds of popular opinion push you off the course of being a peacemaker. Being a peacemaker does not mean that you are an appeaser to all who differ in opinion; it means that the anchor of the Catholic Church is your refuge and lighthouse for others to see. Many people will reject that peace, but you can rest assured that as a father, your attempt will not go unnoticed by God the Father.

Bringing Peace Into Habit and Home

Our older girls have opposite temperaments. Felicity is our introverted melancholic who prefers plenty of solitude outdoors and to be holed up reading books, while Sarah is our boisterous, effervescent, and talkative extrovert who can't stand being alone. As you can imagine, the two of them often argue and bicker. There can be days or even weeks where peace seems nonexistent in our home.

While reading Father Jacques Philippe's book on the Beatitudes, it was clear that peace must begin with us, as parents. We are the authority in the home, and we set the tone for our children's behavior. They are sensitive and pick up on even the subtlest of cues. Father Jacques Philippe believes that peace is the antithesis to both anger and violence in all forms and that the latter can be combatted through daily personal prayer.[18]

---

[18]   Jacques Philippe, *The Eight Doors to the Kingdom*, 184–85.

As parents, we often erroneously believe that vocal prayer is enough to assuage our troubled consciences. Maybe we recite a Rosary without really meditating on the mysteries and accept that as our "daily prayer." We're not discounting the importance of rote vocal prayer. We are merely stating that mental prayer and meditation take us to the depths of our hearts. It is at this deeper level where the fruit of peace is often imparted to us by the Holy Spirit.

Mental prayer is the natural dialogue you have whenever your thoughts or heart are elevated heavenward. Mental prayer is often akin to "spontaneous prayer," or prayer of the heart, because it is not planned or rehearsed. It is like having a natural conversation with a friend. Grow in mental prayer every day. It's best to be attuned to the promptings of the Holy Spirit, who will often inspire you with a deep sense of gratitude or wonder and awe.

Not long ago, I (Jeannie) was having a hectic day. As usual, I'd been running around with the girls from a doctor's appointment to the grocery store to picking up medications to answering phone calls. My heart was restless and anxious. Suddenly, there was a brief patch of quiet, and I saw this moment as an opportunity to collect my thoughts and just breathe. Sarah was at school; Felicity was reading; and Veronica just woke up from a nap.

I took Veronica outside to our backyard swing, and we sat there for maybe ten minutes. It was early spring, and everything was new and fresh. I marveled at the delicate details of the flowering trees and bushes, some redbuds and others dogwoods. The breeze calmed both Veronica and me as she squealed in delight while the swing undulated back and forth in a steady cadence. In that moment, I found myself in prayer. It began as a thought of the beauty of creation and led to a simple prayer of gratitude to God for giving me that moment and the gift of new life.

Mental prayer often leads to meditation too. These do not have to be long, laborious, and intense periods of your day. This type of prayer should be natural spurts of conversation with God interspersed throughout your normal life. But when you practice these types of prayer, you will discover a gentle peace sweep through your body and soul. And your mind will settle into quiet clarity.

Your children, too, will notice this, because you will respond to them differently. You will be more attentive to their needs, listen with love, and discipline with patience. Father Jacques Philippe wrote that "the more one tends toward peace, the more God's grace can act in one's life. As a placid lake mirrors the sun, so a peaceful heart receives the action and motions of the Spirit."[19]

You don't have to march in Washington, DC, or attend a protest in order to be a peacemaker. It's best to begin in your own heart, then practice it in your home with your spouse and children through small but intentional acts of quieting your mind and responding to the frequent invitation to prayer.

---

[19]   Ibid., 187–88.

Action Plan

Toddlers and Preschoolers

For me (Jeannie), the early years are the hardest when it comes to the beatitude of peacemaking. You might feel differently, but I feel constantly tugged and pulled in different directions throughout each day. If you have somehow been blessed with a perfectly compliant child, feel free to skip this section. If, however, you—like me—have been given children who whine, complain, scream when they don't get their way, fight with you and each other, and have adopted "no" as their favorite (or first) word, then please continue.

Teaching the beatitude of peacemaking can be challenging for this age group. Begin by moderating and mediating squabbles between toddlers and their peers or siblings. You can also diffuse potential problems by introducing emotion emojis, which can be printed from online sources. These are little cards that you can laminate and hang up in a prominent place in your home.

When your toddler is feeling angry, upset, sad, or anxious, get that particular card out and say, "You're feeling frustrated right now because you can't play with the toy you want." Over time, likely toward the end of preschool, your child will have a more solid concept of identifying his or her emotions. Next comes emotion regulation, which is a bit tougher.

Peacemaking at this age isn't so much about the spiritual lesson behind selflessness; rather, it's more about teaching a behavior and reinforcing the desired outcome in the home. Conversations will come later.

Elementary Age

School-aged kids can manage a deeper understanding of what being a peacemaker looks like. During the school day, it might mean defending someone who is being left out of a game or made fun of. It might also mean standing up for truth if your child overhears or is actively part of a conversation in which gossip or slander becomes the predominant talking point. Peacemaking can also involve finding time to research different social injustices and learning about how your child or family can become more involved in your parish or community.

Older kids, especially middle-schoolers, are usually in the thick of conflict at home and school. Strife, division, and misunderstanding—usually due to emotional immaturity and the onset of puberty—are rife. It's important to teach your older child about emotion regulation because it is a foundational tenet for becoming a peacemaker. If your child struggles with angry outbursts or verbal assaults, go back to helping him or her identify what emotions are causing the behavior. Try to ask probing questions that might lead you to understand more clearly the impetus for such behavior. Often, it will be something entirely unrelated to the display of emotion.

Part of emotion regulation is being clear about your expectations for showing respect to others. That means no name-calling, no throwing things, no hitting, etc. It also means listening to another person's viewpoint before offering one's own opinion. Tell your child that it's good to be honest and express his feelings, but it's important to do so calmly and respectfully. Give him options to cool off, such as walking away for a few minutes, separating himself from the situation in another room to think it over, taking deep breaths before speaking, etc. Again, emotion regulation at this age is essential to building a peacemaker in your child.

Adolescence

As we have discussed concerning other beatitudes, your teenager might be naturally interested in social justice issues pertaining to peace and unity. These issues will likely be outside of your home, but it's important to return to the source of where harmony should reside—in the home and within the family. If you have a mouthy teen, you can begin at the point of respectful behavior and what your specific expectations for respect are in your household.

At the heart of every young person, though, is usually a cause or mission that strikes her as valuable and worthy of her time. Find out what that is. Don't be afraid to ask your teen questions. At first, it might be messy if most of your conversations involve nagging and nosiness. But if you show genuine interest in what moves her to compassion and persist in finding out what she feels is unfair or unjust in the world, then you can begin a deeper conversation about how she might be able to play a role in helping others overcome their obstacles to peace.

True peacemakers understand that difficult conversations and even confrontations are often necessary before big breakthroughs in communication between diverging parties can occur. On a global scale, that might mean growing in an ecumenical approach to dialogue among Jews, Christians, and Muslims. Your teen may already encounter some of these types of conflicts at school or in certain classes, particularly in social studies. Don't be afraid to ask questions and discuss these current issues that affect her.

To tie everything together, bring in the importance of faith and use examples of saints (see saint profile below) to give your teen inspiration on becoming a courageous person working for peace. Encourage community and parish work that directly involve peacemaking, such as through Catholic Charities or your diocese's Catholic Campaign for Human Development program.

Saint Profile: St. John Paul II

One of the pioneers against Communism in the 1980s and '90s, St. John Paul II was a prolific representation of what it means to be a peacemaker in our modern world. After his visit to his native Poland in 1979, John Paul II saw firsthand how many Poles were longing for liberation from the Marxist influences of Communism. It was the beginning of his crusade to begin writing, speaking, and influencing the world about the negative impacts of Communism from a theological perspective.

Make no mistake: this part of his apostolate was not forceful or based on proselytism. Instead, he built a rapport with world leaders, both political and religious, to begin establishing trust among nations. Above all, his Marian devotion and papal motto, "Totus Tuus" (Totally Yours), strongly propelled his desires to liberate people from the oppressive conditions they faced because of Communist regimes.

The visit to Poland in his early papacy was just the beginning of how John Paul the Great discerned the necessity of promoting and advocating for freedom of all people around the world based on Catholic social teaching's principle of solidarity. Though he and former President Ronald Reagan held different worldviews about why Communism was dangerous, they both worked closely in bringing about the fall of the Berlin Wall in 1989 so that Germany could once again be united.

John Paul II also looked to the East in Asian countries where Communism was pervasive, and through his pastoral gift of peacemaking, he was able to oust Filipino dictator Fernando Marcos from his oppressive position. Many world leaders were humbled and inspired by St. John Paul II's courage, which was expressed in both vulnerable and clear terms.

It is perhaps this great saint who paved the way for his successors to understand more deeply the need for Divine Mercy upon humanity. He certainly lived it well as a diplomat, negotiator, and peacemaker in both personal relationships and worldwide.

As parents, we will not likely make a global impact as a peacekeeper or ambassador for peace. Instead, we can look to St. John Paul II's attributes that made him so successful as a peacemaker and turn to him in prayer and reflection when we seek counsel on difficult issues in our home and family life.

Being a peacemaker as a parent often means mediating petty fights between siblings when they are young (or even older), but it can also mean bringing to light difficult truths that need to be discussed and dealt with, including negative emotions. St. John Paul II was a natural diplomat in that he was able to dialogue with others without coming across as condescending or judgmental. He respected the people with whom he disagreed and listened to their perspective with authentic compassion.

We can also do this when we find ourselves in an uncomfortable situation with our children or social issues they bring to our attention. It's critical that we learn to appreciate vulnerability as a courageous quality, thus building a family and home where discussion is always welcome if it is mutually respectful.

Prayer

Lord, may the prayer of St. Francis of Assisi reign in my heart: Make me an instrument of your peace. Where there is hatred, let me sow love. Where there is injury, pardon. Where there is doubt, faith. Where there is despair, hope. Where there is darkness, light. Where there is sadness, joy. O Divine Master, grant that I may not so much seek to be consoled as to console, to be understood as to understand, to be loved as to love; for it is in giving that we receive, it is in pardoning that we are pardoned, and it is in dying that we are born to eternal life. Amen.

CHAPTER 8

Blessed Are They Who Are Persecuted, for Their Reward Will Be Great in Heaven

Martyrdom is the occasion of our most powerful experience of the Spirit's help.

—Father Jacques Philippe[20]

Jeannie

Persecution is likely one of the most difficult afflictions we will face in our earthly lifetime. Everyone experiences betrayal, false accusations, and other humanly hurts that wound to the core of our being. As parents, we might want to shield our kids from heartaches and rejection, but we know that part of life involves knowing how to face such difficulties with humility and charity.

---

20   Jacques Philippe, *The Eight Doors to the Kingdom*, 206.

When I think of this beatitude, I consider all of the interior suffering that every heart has endured to some degree. Sometimes our suffering is self-imposed, but persecution is not. When we are maligned, mocked, or misunderstood because of our faith, it is not our fault. To be treated unjustly and to be humiliated by people we know and love is not something we seek.

There is a deep sense of rejection and isolation one feels when persecution occurs. Sometimes this rejection is in the form of slander, gossip, and character defamation. We may also face personal insults as our family members and friends notice we are striving to grow in holiness as a family. The spiritual chasm that often results between a life lived radically for the Lord and a life lived for oneself can be paralyzing and ostracizing.

How can we then be consoled when such trials befall us? What about when they happen to our children? We all know that their innocence will be shattered at some point, and they, too, will become jaded by something or someone sooner than we'd like to think. While it's not always helpful to repeat clichés to ourselves or others, such as, "Everything happens for a reason" or "Try to look at the positives," we can maintain hope in the face of adversity. We can journey with Jesus, clinging to him evermore. And we can be assured of the promise we have in heaven one day.

Of course, that's not so easy to live, let alone explain to a crestfallen child. When I was about six years old, I experienced my first betrayal of friendship. My closest friend lived right around the block from my house, and she had moved out of town because of her father's job transfer. We became pen pals, and I awaited her first phone call with bated breath.

When I answered the phone, however, I heard trepidation in her voice. She frankly and decisively explained that we could no longer keep in contact and our friendship was over. How could this be, coming from a young girl? I cried and pleaded with her to reconsider, but she explained that her mother wanted her to meet other kids in their local area.

That betrayal stung for quite a long time. It wasn't that I didn't have any other friends, and she certainly did too, but I felt something so beautiful had been crushed without warning or cause. The wounds of such sorrow did not heal quickly.

Our children, too, will likely experience something similar. Maybe it won't be a friend who outright rejects them, but it could be social isolation on the playground, finding out that someone they trusted was spreading rumors about them at school, and so forth. How can we authentically live out this beatitude so that when persecution does become the uninvited visitor to our family, we can help our kids face it with fortitude?

Something we have tried to instill in our daughters' minds from a young age is the concept of "offering it up." Most of us who are cradle Catholics are probably rolling our eyes right now because "offering it up" is definitely one of those Catholic clichés! Yet it puts into perspective that our struggles are transitory and can be used for some greater good, even something we cannot foresee or understand.

Felicity is particularly sensitive to those who are left out or feeling sad. She notices people who are struggling, and she asks me how she can help them. Sometimes I tell her she can talk to the person if it is in a social situation, making the other child feel welcome and included. But many times, her concerns are more global: the persecuted Christians in the Middle East, the poor and starving orphans of third-world countries, and so on. In those cases, I tell her she can offer up the minor and major irritations or struggles that come her way, giving them to Jesus and praying for those whose plight she wants to assuage so badly.

In this way, it seems that we are able to participate in alleviating the sufferings of the Mystical Body of Christ. When we feel left out or when our kids are hurt by their friends, they endure a small segment of persecution that the poor or marginalized experience. While not an apples-to-apples analogy, there is some sense of strength we gain and a glimmer of hope when we are able to hand over our own sufferings to Jesus and allow him to dispense the pain as love for others we may never meet in this life.

This beatitude is best when lived out on a daily basis. In our family, we say to the girls when they start complaining about their food or doing chores, "Offer it up." It's these small acts of mortification that prepare us for the greater persecutions we will endure. And, as we well know, the small acts we sacrifice to Jesus with heroic love are always efficacious.

Our Lady of Victory

One of the Blessed Mother's primary missions is to crush the head of Satan. We see this mission portrayed in various images of her foot smashing the devil's head. Perhaps that is why, under the title Our Lady of Victory, we can turn to her with increased confidence in her ability to defeat Satan's stronghold in our lives.

The reality is that we are all affected by spiritual warfare. In other words, we need Our Lady of Victory now more than ever because we live in an era where the devil and his minions are clearly scouring the earth to destroy souls and families.

Closely associated with the Miraculous Medal and the Immaculate Conception, Our Lady of Victory conquers every falsehood, every lie and deception, every spiritual plague, and every burden that weighs upon us. Perhaps you have teenagers in your family. Our Lady of Victory is an excellent title to invoke her protection for your teen against all forms of evil. If your children are younger, pray to her to safeguard them against the certain pitfalls of temptation toward arguing, selfishness, and materialism that develops in early life.

Look for novena prayers and the Litany to Our Lady of Victory if you need some ideas on how to jumpstart your devotion. Many Catholic bookstores also carry statues, medals, and holy cards with various images of the Blessed Mother.

Regardless of how you go about beginning this devotion, the key is that Mary under this title will help you specifically to conquer threats, temptations, seductions, vice, fear, contradiction, and unkindness—all related to persecution. She will not only protect you and your family but she will also give you courage necessary to face persecution with peace and charity.

Ben

I cannot begin to fathom the courage it takes to face active persecution as a Christian. I've had my share of bullying as a kid and some snide remarks about my faith, but never anything that would put my life in danger just because I am a Catholic and follower of Christ. Blessed are they who are persecuted, indeed! While we may not be able to point to persecution in our own life as Christians, we can be aware of the persecution that goes on throughout the world. Whether in Iraq, Africa, or at the hand of Hindu nationalists in India, to maintain a pulse on the persecution of Christians can help us to pray for them specifically and find heroic courage in our day and age.

We have so many examples in the news of people who have fallen into sin but very few of true virtue and courage in the face of overwhelming odds. I'm sure there are many years to come of hearing stories about persecuted Christians coming out of the Middle East and other hotspots around the globe. As parents, we should make sure that we share these stories with our children, just as we share stories of saints and their lives of difficulty. These modern saints serve as signposts for our own journeys toward holiness and give us a stark reminder of how blessed we are in the Western world.

Although we may be blessed to live where we do, apathy can be just as harmful as persecution. We should guard against indifference in our own lives and be on watch for an apathetic world when it comes to faith in Christ. Apathy can quickly turn into persecution, and we must be constantly watching for this transition. Many attacks on faith start out as "compassion," especially euthanasia and assisted suicide (which are becoming very prevalent in Europe).

The antidote to apathy is zeal, which can be hard to model, especially when we become drowsy with the daily grind. Going from this appointment to that sports practice to this meeting to that club becomes a string of engagements that don't break up the day into any sort of meaningful chunks of time. If we are not zealous about prayer, we cannot be zealous about our faith. I am not perfect at prayer, either, so don't feel as if this author has it all figured out. I don't, but I do know where my weak points are so that I can work on that zeal for God. It takes real effort, and the heaviness that we feel from daily responsibilities will drag us down if we don't fight against this worldly gravity.

A tactic we can use as a parent, which may seem counter-cultural but one that I've used successfully, is to say "no" to activities. I'm not saying withdraw from everything, but use the word "no" to protect your prayer time, Mass, and other church-centered activities. Be protective of time at Eucharistic Adoration and with the family so that you can model to your children the importance of a Christ-centered life.

By being selective about our time and how it is used, we show our children what is important and what is worth fighting for in our family life. This is how we build the foundation for courageous children to be examples for others in the face of persecution. I pray that persecution does not touch our families, but there's always a chance that it can, given our current culture and the hostility towards God in some circles. Blessed are the persecuted, and we must pray for them, prepare as if we will be persecuted, and strengthen our families with a Christ-centered life.

How St. Joseph's Example Helps Us Handle Persecution

It's nothing new, but persecution of Christians seems to creep closer to home every day. In seemingly distant places, like Africa and the Middle East, we see Christians martyred and sold into slavery. How hard it must have been for St. Joseph to take the Holy Family into Egypt when he knew he was traveling to a hostile land, which had long previously persecuted the Hebrews! We can draw a similar parallel with modern persecutions by imagining if God had asked any of us to travel to a distant land out of obedience. It would certainly be a hard sell, especially as a father who is geared to protect and defend.

As fathers, we must bear two things in mind: first, that obedience to God takes priority over our own wants and desires; and second, that it is better to submit to evil than commit it. If we are obedient to God, then our roles as husbands and fathers will be blessed, even though we most certainly will be stretched by God in all areas of our life. It is also better to be courageous and bear evil than it is to commit it because of our own pride.

St. Joseph trusted God completely and was willing to bear hardship and evil in order to fulfill that obedience. How strong of an example is this for us all and how easily I can say that I have not followed this example as well as I should.

If St. Joseph had not trusted God to flee to an alien land, then Jesus would have been caught in the massacre of the Holy Innocents. By bearing an apparent evil of traveling to a hostile country, he avoided the actual evil of massacre and saved Jesus so that he could complete his reason for coming into our world.

Once again, suffering apparent evils or even *actual* evils has purpose and meaning, even if we do not see these purposes in the moment. As a father, there will be difficult decisions for your family and always lots of prayer to discern what is the right course of action. Constantly petitioning the Holy Spirit to guide you as a father will never lead you down the wrong path. Just be sure to be open to the promptings of the Holy Spirit and resist fear, since fear will never lead you to God's will.

Persecution: Bringing Mortification Into the Heart and Home

This beatitude, of any, is the one most of us cringe at when reading or pondering. Who wants to seek persecution in his or her life? We know that there are martyrs all over the world in the truest sense: those who are literally handing over their lives because of their refusal to apostatize. But martyrdom can happen in another form.

Perhaps you've heard of the "red" and "white" martyrdom concept. St. Maximillian Kolbe is known to have seen the Blessed Mother, who offered him either the red martyrdom of giving his life or the white martyrdom of persecution. He chose both.

Even if we are not asked to shed our blood for the sake of Jesus, we will be asked to give something of ourselves—great things. Therefore, most of us will undergo the white martyrdom, or the crucifixion of the heart, which can take on many forms. For example, persecution may mean being overlooked for a job promotion. It may mean being ignored at a social gathering. Perhaps it is outright mockery when people find out you are Catholic.

Father Jacques Philippe explains that this persecution should not be a reason for despondency, but rather of celebration! "The prospect of persecution, far from being a cause of worry or sadness, should be a source of trust (in the faithfulness and help of God) and even joy."[21] If we live this beatitude well, we will understand how this joy in the midst of persecution unfolds in our families.

Regardless of the form of persecution, we can live a life of this beatitude every day through the means of mortification. By Thomistic definition, mortification is actually a sub-virtue of the cardinal virtue of fortitude. Quite simply, it means we are willing to experience suffering and are not afraid of it. If fortitude as an overall virtue means we must be willing to "engage the arduous" (St. Thomas Aquinas again), then mortifications are specific ways we can either accept the suffering that comes to us through God's permission or choose to make sacrifices for our souls and those of our children's souls.

In our home, offering up small sacrifices is commonplace. Our daughters tend to complain at the slightest discomfort, whether it's environmental temperature, strange new food

---

21   Ibid., 202.

tastes, or having to wait their turn for something exciting. As a result, we have incorporated the concept of mortification by explaining that each time they refrain from complaining and instead offer the little suffering to Jesus, they are growing in virtue.

As explained in the previous chapter, it's tough to truly live out the now-cliched offer-it-up suggestion many of us learned from childhood, but it is possible. Another way is to make each day a mini-Lent. "Give up" something each day, like dessert after dinner, screen time, or even gently used toys and clothing that can be donated monthly. Whatever your family decides, remember that mortification is a method of purifying our souls because we are denying our senses and flesh some comfort or pleasure as a prayer. In turn, the Holy Spirit is freer to move in us and refine the virtues we most lack.

Action Plan

Toddlers and Preschoolers

Very young children will likely not understand the concept of persecution, but they will feel sad or hurt when they are being excluded or ignored. Preschoolers in particular might experience this treatment at school. When Felicity was in preschool, she had a classmate who picked on her nearly every day. When I'd pick her up from school, she was almost in tears on a regular basis. I'd ask her what happened, and she'd tell me that this girl would growl at her, push her out of the way when Felicity was doing an art project, laugh in her face when Felicity was upset or frustrated, and on and on.

I first told Felicity that she might not know what was going on in this girl's life. Maybe something upsetting was happening to her at home. Then I explained how important it is to start over each day with a fresh attitude and perspective. She didn't have to be friends with this girl, but I wanted Felicity to try to be kind despite the negative response she was getting. I encouraged her to smile, say hello, and just be polite.

Something along these lines might be helpful if you have a highly sensitive child like I do. Sensitivity can truly be a gift if it is cultivated in such a way that it begets compassion and empathy. Part of fostering empathy in a very young child is explaining that we don't always understand what people who are mean to us are going through in their lives. This understanding gives your child the ability to act more graciously to one who might have an unrequited vendetta against him or her.

Elementary Age

Growing pains are never enjoyable. Kids in elementary school probably feel awkward, self-conscious, and timorous about at least one aspect of themselves or their abilities. Even overly confident kids are usually covering for some insecurity they haven't revealed to anyone. Children who are the victims of persecution are often seen as sensitive by their peers. Their areas of vulnerability have been exposed in some way, which stronger personalities might interpret as a sign of weakness. In turn, they prey upon that perceived weakness.

If you haven't already, start talking to your child about Jesus's passion. You can download a kids' Stations of the

Cross that you might consider praying on Fridays (even when it's not Lent). Explain that we can always turn to Jesus when we are feeling betrayed or judged by others, when we feel lost and alone, and when we are hurt or misunderstood. Help your child develop a devotion to the Sacred Heart of Jesus. Introduce Eucharistic Adoration. This is a vital time to bring your child's wounded heart to Jesus so that Jesus will become his main confidant. Then turning to the Lord in prayer will be a natural response when he feels slighted by someone.

As a family, you can discuss with discretion about the persecuted Christians who face martyrdom today. Pray for them each night. Talk about how the saints displayed heroic courage in the face of extreme persecution that often led to their deaths and how we can emanate that courage when we are faced with our own hardships.

Adolescence

If there's ever a time in life most of us would rather not return to, it's high school years. Teens are exploring healthy ways to communicate with each other. They are learning about relationships every day, and they often find that friendships vacillate and people change over time. For the sensitive and loyal child, these occurrences will be troublesome. Facing the pain of losing a friend or even romantic interest might be his or her first experience of deep emotional pain.

Give your teen a prayer journal with some colorful pens. Encourage him or her to use it as a space to pour out his or her heart to God through drawing, coloring, doodling, writing—whatever allows him or her to connect with God in a meaningful and healing way. The journal is helpful because teens don't often open up about their most private feelings and thoughts, but if they have a space that can be solely shared with God, it may bring about consolation when heartbreak inevitably happens. (This was also a suggestion in an earlier chapter; journals are versatile and therapeutic.)

Encourage your child to befriend those who might also be experiencing persecution—maybe for their religion, race, or disability. It could be any number of reasons why someone at your child's school is being ostracized. Now is a perfect age to discuss world conflicts and introduce various saints (see the saint profile below for an example) who endured persecution with great courage and conviction. These discussions also foster empathy and may naturally lead into your child to develop the spiritual gifts of counsel, wisdom, or knowledge.

Prayer life is essential to managing the poverty of loneliness and the sense of being forsaken. Find a teen devotional on the subject of loss and sorrow. Explore different forms of prayer as a family, and always encourage your teen to turn to Jesus, his guardian angel, and the saints for consolation.

Saint Profile: St. Thomas More

We can learn a lot about persecution from a plethora of saints, countless numbers even. Today, we know there are Christians all over the world who are being martyred for their faith in Jesus. Ben and I really like St. Thomas More, not necessarily because there aren't better examples of saints who were persecuted, but because More's courage during an incredibly tumultuous time in the history of the Church and the world exemplifies what it means to face judgment from humankind, yet remain faithful to God despite imminent death.

Thomas More was a married father whose vocation also included being a lawyer and councilor to King Henry VIII. A brilliant scholar and prolific philosopher, Renaissance humanist, and writer, More deemed his position as the king of England's advisor to be an honorable one, one that he maintained with the sincerest integrity.

In the midst of More's life and work, the Protestant Reformation surged to the forefront of religious strife in the early sixteenth century, and More openly opposed it. He viewed the schism as a threat against the Church and society as a whole, claiming that "Luther's call to destroy the Catholic Church [was] a call to war."[22] At the same time the Protestant Reformation occurred, Henry VIII decided to break away from the Catholic Church when he was not granted permission to divorce his wife after she failed to bear him an heir. Furious, he chose to form his own church, the Anglican church, which would allow divorce.

More opposed the king's decision, and as a result, King Henry VIII felt More was directly opposing his regime. More knew that opposing the king would lead to a formidable consequence, but his bravery to remain faithful to the Catholic Church led him to sainthood through martyrdom.

---

[22]   Gerard B. Wegemer, *Thomas More: A Portrait of Courage* (Scepter, 2012), p. 136.

Perhaps St. Thomas More is such a remarkable example of facing persecution with heroic faith because he did not shrink from conflict. While he didn't seek out conflict, he faced it and named it what it was—heresy. Using such strong and clear language did not endear him to those around him. But More didn't impulsively oppose the Protestants or King Henry; he thoughtfully and carefully discerned that God was calling him to support the supremacy of the Roman Catholic pope, not just in good faith or silently in his heart, but openly.

Many times, we will face various forms of persecution, sometimes in our marriages, in the workplace, throughout our extended families, in our neighborhoods, and so on. Persecution doesn't simply mean we are ignored or ridiculed; it means we face backlash when we defend our Faith to others.

Our children, too, may encounter harsh criticism, judgment, or ostracization from their peer groups or among friends when they decide to share their faith in God. Even if other people share a vague belief in God, they might cringe when they hear our children are from a practicing Catholic family. And that will feel like betrayal to our children.

But what we must do as parents is similar to what St. Thomas More had to do: respond with dignity and diplomacy. We can teach our children to be proud of their faith and to share it with others when the occasion arises. None of us should fear the possibility of persecution, though it does wound our pride and may cause us to clam up in future circumstances where God is asking us to speak up.

So, too, must we patch the wounds that our kids experience when they are persecuted. We can share the story of

St. Thomas More's incredible steadfast commitment to the Catholic Church and how he bravely faced his own execution with holy character and patient perseverance. Though we and our children will likely never face literal martyrdom, as St. Thomas More did, we will experience the martyrdom of loneliness, rejection, and betrayal based on our religious convictions. How we handle such heartaches determines how ready we are to receive our reward in heaven.

Prayer

Lord, you told us that our reward would be great in heaven if we faced persecution because of your name. Many times, I find it hard to be the kind of Christian I long to be— brave, never afraid of defending the Faith, strong, and forgiving. Yet so often I have encountered people who judge me because of my faith, my parenting style, the way I do my job, and my personal values. Help me endure such treatment without adopting a victim mentality or superiority complex. Instead, teach me to endure all my trials with patience and humility so that I might teach my children to do the same. Lead me as a parent in praying for my children as they experience the hardships of heartbreak. May we all turn to you as an example and stronghold when we are weary and discouraged. Jesus, I trust in you. Amen.

Conclusion

Beatitude is a possession of all things held to be good, from which nothing is absent that a good desire may want. Perhaps the meaning of beatitude may become clearer to us if it is compared with its opposite. Now the opposite of beatitude is misery. Misery means being afflicted unwillingly with painful sufferings.

—St. Gregory of Nyssa

Our ultimate mission as parents is to help our children get to heaven one day. When we strive for holiness in our daily lives, enduring the struggles we face within and without, we pave the way to heaven as being approachable and attainable for our kids. It's important for us to remember that holiness is possible for all of us. We often don't realize it, but holiness includes all the little, hidden deeds we give to the Lord throughout our daily lives that add up to greatness.

It may seem that we are far from the path to heaven some days. We often hang our heads at the end of a tough day or even week, wondering how we got it all wrong. The girls might be constantly bickering, refusing to take turns and share toys, whining and grousing about meals, or obstinately disobeying us. Sometimes it's a combination of these. We feel as if all we are doing is managing one misbehavior after another, doling out consequences that seem interminable.

But then we gather for evening prayer as a family, which includes petitions and a Rosary or Divine Mercy chaplet. This quiet time centers us and helps us focus on our day. It often elicits conversations with the girls that they initiate, including remorse for their behavior and prayers to Jesus and the saints that they will try better tomorrow.

The point is that living our primary vocation as wives, mothers, husbands, and fathers necessarily entails diving into the mess and chaos and mistakes without giving up. We must persevere through the travails of parenthood, even when we are on the cusp of defeat, and remember that it's never too late to begin again.

St. Gregory of Nyssa's quotation reminds us that when we work toward our sanctification using the Beatitudes as a guidepost, we will discover huge transformations in our lives. We will see spiritual growth in our children and holiness in our marriages. We will discover that our family is stronger, more resilient, and capable of achieving great things for God.

Greatness never comes without a price. So don't expect this path to be simple, easy, and smooth sailing. It won't be. It will be confusing at times, maybe even seemingly unrealistic. But the point is that we get up after we fall, and we help our children get back up too. We do not give into the cultural pressures of acquiescing to laziness and apathy. Instead, the Beatitudes inspire us to do more, or rather to *be* more, than we are today.

When our children notice that fire in our hearts, they will ask about it. And we can demonstrate humility to them when we mess up by apologizing, asking for forgiveness, and explaining that people who love each other sometimes don't agree. Some healthy conflict is good for kids to witness, especially when they learn how the conflict is resolved through mutually respectful communication.

The final point: just begin. Begin *today*. Don't wait for tomorrow or some utopian opportune moment, because it won't arrive. The present moment is where the Holy Spirit operates. Trust that God has given you the grace to parent your children and ask him to show you where to start. Use this book to inspire and encourage you, but don't be bogged down by specifics. Every family dynamic is different, and these ideas are only suggestions to give you a boost in what might work for your particular family situation.

And foster the spiritual gifts you notice developing in your children. For some, it might be compassion for the poor. For others, it might be hospitality. Whatever the case may be, the Beatitudes act as a beacon for us, leading our hearts toward heaven by how we live and what we believe. Above all, remember that God's grace is sufficient for you, and his grace will always compensate for your lack. Don't be afraid to do great things for him.

Discussion Questions

Chapter 1: Blessed Are the Poor in Spirit

1. What does "the poor are our teachers" mean to you?
2. How can you seek to be poor yourself?
3. How are we like the poor among us?
4. How is being poor in spirit related to simplicity and surrender?
5. In what ways do your children exhibit poverty of spirit?
6. How can poverty of spirit allow God to protect and provide for you?
7. How is simplicity the "intersection of thought, obedience, and action" in your life?
8. What does it mean for you to move from selfish living to generous giving?

Chapter 2: Blessed Are They Who Mourn

1. How can you help your children understand the merit of their suffering?
2. How can suffering help you grow in the virtue of fortitude?
3. What does it mean to you to "suffer well"?
4. How can you "persevere through dryness in

relationships, life circumstances, and prayer"?

5. What does it mean to be comfortable with the discomforts in life?

6. How can you turn toward "action in prayer" rather than "words of complaint" in times of mourning?

7. In what way(s) can you accompany others who are suffering?

8. What does "suffering can be lived with joy" mean to you?

Chapter 3: Blessed Are the Meek

1. How is meekness the foundation of humility in your life?

2. What does it mean to you for meekness to be the virtue that opens our hearts to grace?

3. How is meekness the "characteristic attribute of the Holy Spirit's action" in your life?

4. How do you moderate your anger through meekness?

5. In what ways was Jesus meek? How can you imitate his meekness?

6. Why is meekness not weakness?

7. Explain how sensitivity, receptivity, compassion, and forgiveness are all related to meekness in your understanding.

8. How can you relate obedience to meekness with your children?

Chapter 4: Blessed Are They Who Hunger and Thirst for Righteousness

1. What is your deepest spiritual hunger or thirst?
2. How can you mete out discipline to your children with both justice and mercy?
3. What does it mean to you for Mary to "speed up the hour of grace" in your life?
4. How does hungering and thirsting for righteousness fulfill a need rather than a desire in your life?
5. How can you encourage your kids to seek God's righteousness?
6. Describe a time when waiting for God's justice bore fruit in your life.
7. How does "demanding justice lead to injustice"?
8. How is holy righteousness different from being right?

Chapter 5: Blessed Are the Merciful

1. How is mercy "love in action"?
2. Who is/has been the "face of mercy" in your life?
3. How is mercy a "communal action" in your life experience?
4. In what way(s) does forgiveness help you become more merciful to others?
5. How can you extend mercy to yourself in difficult situations?
6. How can frequent confession soften your heart to God's mercy?

7. In what way(s) can you point out your children's gifts and strengths as an act of mercy?
8. What are some Corporal or Spiritual Works of Mercy you can adopt as a family?

Chapter 6: Blessed Are the Pure of Heart

1. How can your children teach you to return to innocence?
2. How did your heart change when you became a parent?
3. How can you foster devotion to the Immaculate Conception in your family?
4. In what way(s) can you maintain purity of thought through custody of the mind?
5. What fruits have you noticed as you grow in purity of heart?
6. How can St. Joseph help you conquer impurity in your life?
7. What are ways you can "praise and bless God" more every day?
8. What does "everything is grace" mean to you?

Chapter 7: Blessed Are the Peacemakers

1. How are you a peacemaker as a parent?
2. How is peace different than the absence of conflict or war?
3. How is peace related to clarity of mind in your life?
4. What are ways peace can come into your life through greater mental prayer?

5. What are ways you can work for peace in your community?

6. What does "the peace that surpasses all understanding" mean to you?

7. How can greater trust in God foster peace in your family?

8. How does being a peacemaker keep you grounded?

Chapter 8: Blessed Are They Who Are Persecuted

1. How can you teach your kids to offer their suffering to Jesus?

2. How can you be more aware of Christian persecution in the world and pray for them?

3. How does apathy turn into persecution?

4. What does it mean to "better to submit to evil than to commit it"?

5. How can you sacrifice more of yourself and your time to God?

6. What does joy in the midst of suffering mean to you?

7. What can you "give up" as a family?

8. When you hear the phrase, "Everyone is suffering a battle you know nothing about," how are you led to greater compassion for those who hurt you or your kids?

About the Authors

Ben and Jeannie Ewing live with their three daughters and son in northern Indiana. Jeannie is a Catholic spirituality writer who writes about moving through grief, the value of redemptive suffering, and how to wait for God's timing fruitfully. Her books include *Navigating Deep Waters*, *From Grief to Grace*, *A Sea Without A Shore*, *For Those Who Grieve*, and *Waiting with Purpose*. She is a frequent guest on Catholic radio and contributes to several online and print Catholic periodicals. For more information, please visit her website jeannieewing.com.